RAISED-BED GARDENING
FOR BEGINNERS

RAISED-BED GARDENING
for beginners

Everything You Need to Know
to Start and Sustain
a Thriving Garden

Tammy Wylie

**ROCKRIDGE
PRESS**

Rockridge Press publishes its books in a variety of electronic and print formats. Some content that appears in print may not be available in electronic books, and vice versa.

TRADEMARKS: Rockridge Press and the Rockridge Press logo are trademarks or registered trademarks of Callisto Media Inc. and/ or its affiliates, in the United States and other countries, and may not be used without written permission. All other trademarks are the property of their respective owners. Rockridge Press is not associated with any product or vendor mentioned in this book.

Cover and Interior Designer: Jami Spittler
Art Manager: Sue Bischofberger
Editor: Vanessa Ta
Production Manager: Oriana Siska
Production Editor: Melissa Edeburn
Illustration: © 2019 Tom Bingham

Photography: © Rawpixel.com/shutterstock, p. ii; © jgolby/shutterstock, pp. x-xi; © Africa Studio/ shutterstock, p. 62; © Isabel Eve/shutterstock, p. 64; © Svetlana-Cherruty/iStock, p. 66; © Vitalii Marchenko/shutterstock, p. 68; © Norman Chan/ shutterstock, p. 70; © pidjoe/iStock, p. 72; © GomezDavid/iStock, p. 74; © inalex/shutterstock, p. 76; © synchR/shutterstock, p. 78; © Multistock/ shutterstock, p. 80; © lovelyday12/shutterstock, p. 82; © Orest lyzhechka/shutterstock, p. 84; © Svetlana Foote/shutterstock, p. 86; © CTatiana/ shutterstock, p. 88; © Altinosmanaj/iStock, p. 90; © bentaboe/iStock, p. 92; © Bohbeh/ shutterstock, p. 94; © Milosz_G/shutterstock, p. 96; © Inga Gedrovicha/shutterstock, p. 98; © duckycards/iStock, p. 100; © Charivna_Divchina/ shutterstock, p. 102; © azure/shutterstock, p. 104; © Kingarion/shutterstock, p. 106; © Jane McLoughlin/shutterstock, p. 108; © Abrym/ shutterstock, p. 110; © Zhukovskaya Elena/ shutterstock, p. 112; © Kedsirin.J/shutterstock, p. 114; © Tom Meaker/iStock, p. 116; © Cora Mueller/shutterstock, p. 118; © Mathia Coco/ shutterstock, p. 122.

Hardcover ISBN: 978-1-63807-993-4 |
Paperback ISBN: 978-1-64152-509-1 |
eBook ISBN: 978-1-64152-510-7

R0

INTRODUCTION

I was introduced to gardening at a very young age. My favorite picture is of me with a shovel and my Dad with a rake working in our garden. I was two years old. And, I am happy to say, gardening has stuck with me throughout my lifetime. I take such immense pleasure in planting a seed or a seedling, nurturing it, and watching it grow. The best part is when you walk out into the garden to decide what you will have for dinner that night. You have a veritable fresh produce aisle right in your own backyard—not to mention the fresh flowers for a centerpiece and the fresh herbs to add flavor to your meal.

The way I garden has changed since my first attempts. The first house I bought had plenty of land for a garden. I borrowed a front-tine rototiller and dug up the garden on my own. Have you ever used a tiller? The front-tine models are the worst. They rock and roll—and you go right along with them. Then came my introduction to the rear-tine tiller, which is a little bit easier to handle. Whew!

And, finally, a neighbor introduced me to raised-bed gardening. He used a free-form mound configuration, without any edging or border around his beds. I was intrigued by the idea and started doing some research into this new way of gardening.

The next year I put in four square raised-bed gardens with wood frames. That change made all the difference for me. Raised beds are absolutely the best way to garden. I have been growing with this method for more than 30 years now. You do not need a tiller and can build the beds in a convenient configuration. Compared with conventional gardening, raised-bed gardening offers a higher yield in less space and requires less weeding. You will learn all the benefits of raised-bed gardening throughout this book.

You can reap the benefits of growing your own food—even if you live on a small property, rent your home, or only have a balcony or patio. In this book, I will guide you through decisions about the location, size, and construction of your raised bed and about which crops to plant, whether to start with seeds or seedlings (sprouted seeds), and when and how to harvest.

Get ready to dig in!

||||||||||||||||||||||||||||||||||||||||||||||||||||||||||||||||||

CHAPTER ONE

PLANNING YOUR GARDEN

Congratulations on deciding to grow your plants using raised-bed gardens—the absolute best way to grow! This chapter introduces you to some of the basic decisions you will need to make. Planning ahead is essential. You want to give your plants the environment they need to grow to ensure a healthy, productive harvest. You may start preparing your ground in fall for next spring's growing season, or you may even decide to grow some winter crops. With proper planning and preparation, you will have a raised-bed garden that is the envy of your neighborhood.

LOCATION

Location is one of the most important decisions you will make when starting your raised-bed garden. You must give your plants the proper conditions they need to thrive, so keep in mind these important considerations about location.

If you have limited space, don't worry. Place your raised beds on your patio if you have sufficient light there. Raised-bed gardening produces comparatively high yields, meaning you get more produce from less space, because of several factors. The soil gets warmer earlier in the year, enabling the plants to grow faster. Plants are placed closer together than when planted in rows, so you have more plants producing. (In traditional gardening, you typically leave 2 to 3 feet between rows. With raised beds, you use this space for planting.) You also create your own soil mix rather than trying to improve existing soil, which contributes to higher yields.

Sun

Most garden vegetables need at least 6 hours of sunshine daily. You want to position your raised beds so as to avoid anything that could cast shadows on them, such as buildings and trees. Those shadows can change with the seasons. If you're choosing your garden location in winter, remember that deciduous trees lose their leaves in winter but have them again in the spring. Insufficient sunlight may lead to stunted plants, slow or no growth, disease, and insects.

Drainage

Raised beds will help you with drainage. Nevertheless, you want your garden to be in an area with good natural drainage. Do not place the beds in low-lying or swampy areas prone to flooding, which may limit access to your garden.

Air Circulation

Your garden needs good air circulation but shouldn't be in an extremely windy area. For example, you do not want to plant your garden directly beside a privacy fence, which will block all the airflow to the plants. If you have ever been in a commercial greenhouse, you may have noticed circulating fans running all the time, mimicking a gentle breeze. Good air circulation is essential to a healthy garden. Your plants need circulation to deter some molds, mildews, and pests as well as to develop strong stems and remain generally healthy. If you see your plants gently swaying in the breeze, you have located your garden in the proper location.

Water

You want your garden to be near a water source, such as a spigot with a hose. Soil in raised beds warms faster than soil at ground level. Therefore, the soil in raised beds also dries out faster. Multiple daily trips with a watering can are not practical. First-time gardeners will probably prefer to run a hose to their gardens. More experienced gardeners can consider the convenient but more expensive route: running water lines and placing a frost-free hydrant directly in the garden. Get your garden established before you consider this option.

Logistics

If you live in a subdivision with a homeowners' association (HOA), check with the association before building your garden. Most HOAs have strict rules regarding anything in the front yard. Some even have rules regarding backyard gardens.

Take your time choosing a location. Visualize it in your mind and consider making a drawing showing your proposed spot, along with nearby buildings and natural amenities such as trees and shrubbery. Alternatively, purchase a bundle of surveyor's stakes (at your local home store or lumber-yard) and use them to mark the corners of your beds. Wrap a piece of rope or twine around the stakes to see the bed area and your pathway. If you are planning multiple beds, lay them out to see how the pathways fit. Walk through and think about how everything works together.

SIZE

Now that you have determined the best location for your garden, you should decide on the proper size. Remember, you don't need to put in a big garden to get a big yield with raised beds. More crops will fit in a raised-bed garden than in a traditional garden (see page 2), so you will not need as much space to grow the same amount of food. Your beds can be as small as 3 feet by 3 feet; they can be as long as you like but no more than 4 feet wide.

Consider how many crops you want to start with. For example, if you are planting tomatoes, they should be spaced 3 feet apart. If you are planting in a 4-by-4-foot bed, you would place one tomato plant in each corner, being sure to leave room for the support cages.

If you are a beginner gardener, I suggest starting small. Pick just a few of your favorite things to eat fresh, and make sure they are feasible to grow in your climate. You may choose to start with only one bed. A single bed will be easy to maintain and prevent you from becoming burned out by too much work the first year. Add one or two beds each year if you have adequate space and sunlight.

Bed Width

One of the best features of raised-bed gardening is that you can avoid walking on your garden surface, which leads to soil compaction—a down-side of traditional gardening. Loose soil means healthier, stronger, more productive plants. The most important factor in sizing your bed is determining which dimensions will allow you to work the bed without walking on it.

Typical dimensions are a 4-by-4-foot bed for an adult and a 30-by-30-inch or even 3-by-3-foot bed for a child or teen. To determine what size is comfortable for you to work, kneel down and reach out as far as is comfortable and place a marker, such as a stone, in that spot. Don't try to stretch as far as you possibly can. Just reach to the spot where you would be able to pull weeds, pick crops, and pinch tops off plants. Measure the distance from your marker to the spot where you are kneeling and double that measurement. Make a square that size for your garden bed. For example, if you can easily reach out 2 feet, double that distance to 4 feet and build a 4-by-4-foot bed. Remember, the bed should fit you.

Depth

You will also need to decide the depth of the raised bed. Consider what will be growing during all seasons. You may have plants with shallow roots during part of the year, but if you are growing root crops, such as carrots and parsnips, you will need a bed deep enough for them to grow. A Danvers carrot—a common varietal—will grow 6 to 8 inches long. A parsnip can grow as long as 12 inches. The minimum depth for a raised bed should be 6 inches, but make the bed as high as you want (as long as you can fill the entire bed with soil).

Walkways

You will want a walkway between beds that is large enough to accommodate any tools you will need to work in your garden. If you like to use a wheelbarrow or a garden cart, make sure your walkways are wide enough for them to fit.

Shape

Raised-bed gardens do not have to be square. Because you are building the bed yourself, it's not a problem if you want a rectangular configuration or some other configuration that will fit the space you have available for your garden. My garden has four rows that are 4 feet wide and 60 feet long. (I would never recommend this much space for a beginner.) Most crops are planted in two rows, each about 1 foot in along the 60-foot sides. Some crops, such as corn, onions, and garlic, have multiple plants across a row. This size is more than adequate to provide plentiful fresh food for two people as well as extra food to share with friends and neighbors and to preserve for winter.

PLANTS

Okay—now it's time to get serious about which plants to grow. This choice is just as important as garden location and size. Your first consideration should be what you like to eat. Don't waste your valuable time and real estate growing something no one in your family will eat. Plant only small quantities of new-to-you vegetables, herbs, or flowers. When weighing your choices, also take into account the space in the bed. If you have only one 4-by-4-foot bed, your growing area is limited.

Keep a Journal

I keep a journal detailing what I have grown, how many plants I have put in, and where in the garden I planted them. I also keep notes on how well the plants produce vegetables and how they taste, unless they are old standbys. In year one, you won't have that history available, but you should still draw out a plan, figure out how much space you have, and determine the best spot in the garden for each plant, then document all that information.

Companion Planting

Use the companion chart (see pages 10-11) to learn which vegetables like to be near one another and which ones don't. One natural pairing is corn, which needs a lot of nitrogen, and beans, which are nitrogen fixers (plants that turn unusable nitrogen in the air into usable nitrogen). Some crops should not be grown together because they attract the same pests or diseases. Make sure the plants you choose to grow together have comparable needs. You don't want sun-loving plants (which include most vegetables) and shade-loving plants together.

Proper Season

Make sure you plant during the proper season. See the Resources section on page 125 for information on how to contact your local agricultural extension office. Agricultural extension programs, a free service of the United States Department of Agriculture (USDA), offer education about gardening, farming, and other areas of agriculture. Local agents should be able to tell you specific varieties that will grow well in your area. Many states publish that information, along with a planting schedule for each crop.

Proper Zone

You should learn your planting zone. The USDA provides a map for gardeners to determine which plants will do best in various climates. Find a map of plant hardiness zones on page 126.

Spacing

The beauty of a raised-bed garden is that seeds can be planted much closer together than in a conventional garden, where plant rows generally must be kept 3 feet apart. The best approach is to mark off a section of the bed and dedicate it to whichever plant you choose. If the seed packet recommends that seeds be planted 3 inches apart, you can place the seeds 3 inches apart in all directions, creating a block rather than a row of plants.

Keep in mind the quantity of each plant you are planting. For example, if you plant 100 lettuces, they will all be ready to harvest around the same time. Are you ready to eat 100 heads of lettuce within a week? Probably not. Keep the number of plants realistic or stagger your planting dates to prolong your harvest.

Taller Plants

Consider the size of the grown plants. Tall plants are best planted on the north side of a raised-bed garden to avoid casting shadows on shorter ones. Some plants may need trellises as they grow. Allow enough room for these supports and make sure, again, to avoid casting shadows.

Flowers and Herbs

Don't forget to plant herbs and flowers. Nasturtiums are edible flowers, and marigolds help keep pests away. Herbs like basil are a great addition to salads, marinades, and meats. This is your garden. Plant what makes you happy, and plant what you like to eat. Just be sure to plant during the proper season, with the proper spacing.

PLANT FRIENDS AND FOES

Some types of plants are not good companions. If grown together, types with similar nutrient needs may not have those needs met, and some other types may experience pest issues. On the other hand, some plants are good companions, providing each other with something extra they need to grow. The following table lists plants that grow well together and plants that don't.

PLANT	FRIEND*	FOE**	NOTES
Beans Corn Squash or Pumpkin *Grow these three together*	Beans - Eggplant Corn - Cucumbers Squash - Nasturtiums	Beans - Alliums (garlic, leeks, onions) Corn - Tomatoes Squash - Potatoes	Beans, corn, and squash are called the "three sisters." Corn is a natural support for beans and uses a lot of nitrogen. Beans are a nitrogen fixer. Squash has large leaves to block weeds. Corn and tomatoes are susceptible to a common fungus.
Beets	Broccoli Bush beans Cabbage Garlic Kale Lettuce Onions	Pole beans	Pole beans and beets stunt each other's growth.
Cucumbers	Bush beans Cantaloupe Lettuce Radishes	Potatoes	You may get potato blight if you plant cucumbers with potatoes.
Herbs, such as chives, garlic, oregano, rosemary, and thyme	Rosemary - Sage	Rosemary - All other herbs	Plant herbs around other plants in your garden to minimize harmful insects.

* FRIEND Okay to Grow These Plants Together ** FOE Do Not Grow These Plants Together

PLANT	FRIEND*	FOE**	NOTES
Lettuce	Carrots	Cabbage	Lettuce has shallow roots; carrot roots grow deeper in the soil. They do not compete with each other for space.
Onions	Asparagus Broccoli Brussels sprouts Cabbage Kale	Beans Peas	Onions will naturally repel the pests of the cabbage family, such as cabbage worms.
Peas	Carrots Radishes Turnips	Beans Garlic Onions	Peas and beans are not chemically compatible. Planting these together may also lead to an off taste.
Peppers	Basil Carrots Eggplant Onions Parsley Tomatoes	Kohlrabi	Basil will keep thrips, flies, and mosquitoes at bay. These insects can be detrimental to pepper plants.
Potatoes	Beans Corn Peas	Peppers Tomatoes	Potatoes, tomatoes, and peppers are all members of the nightshade family, and, therefore, susceptible to the same diseases.
Tomatoes	Asparagus Basil Marigolds	Corn	Asparagus deters nematodes, which are an issue for tomatoes. Basil repels flies and mosquitoes. Marigolds help keep away tomato hornworms. Corn and tomatoes are susceptible to a common fungus.

* FRIEND Okay to Grow These Plants Together   ** FOE Do Not Grow These Plants Together

CROP ROTATION

Crop rotation is a simple concept: Don't plant the same crops year after year in the same location. If you have enough room, the best practice is to plant your crops in the same location every 4 years, even if you only have one bed. Divide it into quarters and shift your plantings into the next quarter in each season.

Crop rotation helps increase the fertility of your soil, increasing crop yield and decreasing pest infiltration and disease. The grouping of plant types reflects nutrient needs as well as pest and disease risks.

Some plants will deplete all of a certain nutrient and some plants will replenish them. Broccoli, cabbage, corn, and squash can use large amounts of nitrogen. Legumes, such as beans or peas, are nitrogen fixers—they convert atmospheric nitrogen that is unusable by other plants into nitrogen that is usable. If possible, plant legumes in the spot that you planted corn the previous year.

Your garden journal can inform your planting strategy. Not only should you keep notes about the varieties you planted, you should also draw diagrams of where they were planted each year.

Plants are commonly divided into four groups for crop rotation purposes:

1. Leaves: greens, herbs, lettuces—any plant with edible leaves
2. Legumes: beans and peas
3. Roots: beets, carrots, and turnips, for example
4. Vegetables: eggplant, peppers, and tomatoes, for example

CHAPTER TWO

BUILDING STRUCTURES

You have done all your homework. You have studied your yard or other available space to find the perfect location. You have chosen the best size for your needs—at least to start. (Chances are, your garden will become larger at some point if you have the space and time.) You have studied the vegetables you love to eat and have chosen the appropriate plants for the season. What's left? The fun part.

RAISED BEDS

Now it is time to design and build a raised-bed garden to fit your needs and aesthetic. In this chapter you will compare the pros and cons of materials and designs for building your bed. You will look at everything from a 4-by-4-foot box structure to raised beds with legs and raised beds made from recycled materials to custom-designed beds.

Preparing the Area

If you are placing your raised bed in your yard, remove any grass in the area where the bed will be. Use a square shovel and "scrape" off the grass. After it is removed, loosen up the soil by turning it over with a shovel. Dig a minimum of 12 inches deep for good drainage.

Selecting Materials

Select the material for the structure. You may use new materials, but don't forget that recycled materials are also an option. Some possibilities follow.

- Rot-resistant wood, such as cedar and redwood are excellent, albeit expensive, options.

- Concrete blocks are expensive but permanent, and even their holes can be filled with soil for planting.

- Galvanized tin will not rot but has sharp edges that you may want to frame for safety reasons.

Never use railroad ties to build raised beds. They are coated with creosote, which is poisonous. If you are using recycled boards, be sure you know what you have. Any pressure-treated wood that was manufactured prior to

2003 contains arsenic, which is carcinogenic. New copper-treated lumber products are safe for raised beds.

- ◈ Always use stainless steel fasteners to avoid rust from high exposure to moisture and water.

You will need the following supplies to build a 4-by-4-foot raised bed that is 6 inches high:

- ◈ Two 2 × 6 × 8 pressure-treated boards for the sides
- ◈ One 2 × 4 × 8 pressure-treated board for stakes
- ◈ Tape measure
- ◈ Skill saw

- ◈ Drill with screwdriver bit to match your fasteners
- ◈ Screws or other fasteners
- ◈ Framing square
- ◈ Level
- ◈ Sledgehammer

You need all these tools regardless of the size of your bed. Calculate the amount of wood to build a bed in your desired size.

Building the Bed

1. Cut your 2 x 6 boards to length. You will need two 48-inch pieces and two 45-inch pieces.

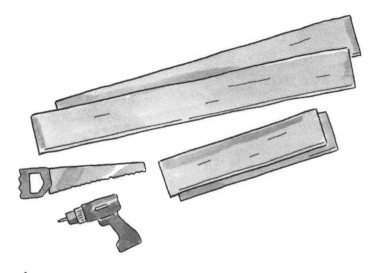

2. Lay them out on a flat surface, as close to the final location as possible, with the face of the 48-inch boards covering the ends of the 45-inch boards.

3. Using 2 screws for each corner, screw through the longer boards into the ends of the shorter boards at each corner.

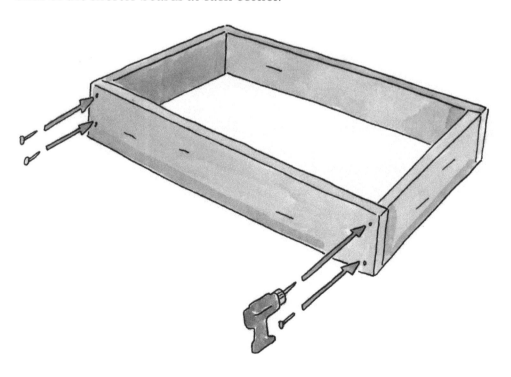

4. If you are placing your beds in your yard, rather than on a porch, complete your site prep work. Remove the grass and work the soil beneath the bed.

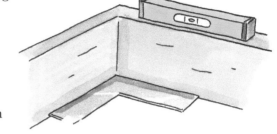

5. Place the bed in its location, making sure it is square and level. To check for squareness, use a framing square in the corners of the bed. Both sides of the framing square should be flat against the side boards of the frame. To check for levelness, place a level on top of the boards. If they are level, the bubble will be centered between the two lines.

6. Cut your 2 x 4 board into four 18-inch stakes with pointed ends. Place one stake in each corner inside the frame. Drive the pointed end into the ground with a sledgehammer until it is flush with the top of your bed frame.

7. Using 2 screws at each corner, screw through the 45-inch board into the stake. You should always have your beds staked down to keep them from shifting.

8. Fill your bed and prepare it for planting.

> **TIP:** If you are building a bed longer than 4 feet, you will need additional stakes—one every 4 feet on the inside of the bed to keep it from bulging when filled with soil. If your bed is bulging, you have not used enough stakes.

ODD-SHAPED STRUCTURES

Building an odd-shaped structure is quite similar to building a square bed, so don't worry if you lack the perfect spot for a 4-by-4-foot raised-bed garden or you prefer a more aesthetically pleasing shape. Your structure's shape doesn't need to abide by any strict rules. I promise the vegetables and flowers will never complain.

Want to execute a star shape? Frame It All (see Resources, page 125) has corner stakes with adjustable angles for the job. This manufacturer's website offers kits and recommendations for various shapes as well as composite boards that are straight and curved. Just keep in mind that you need to be able to reach across your odd-shaped bed to comfortably work it.

If you are creative, use materials such as privacy fence planks or cedar shingles. Such materials are narrow and can be placed close together to make a unique design with odd angles. (Consider lining the bed with heavy polyethylene if you go this route.)

Do you have a feature in your yard you want to build around? If so, you can create any type of geometric shape you prefer. If you want to build a circular bed, consider materials such as circular composite boards or lawn edging made from PVC or a composite material. (Tip: Lawn edging is usually only 4 inches tall, so don't try it for growing tomatoes, potatoes, or root crops. It would, however, be great for lettuces and crops with shallow roots.)

If bending down or kneeling is not possible or is uncomfortable for you, try elevating your raised-bed garden with legs of a height that works for you. Line the bed with a material that allows for drainage and that helps keep the dirt in place. Landscape cloth is an excellent choice.

Even if you envision a simple bed shape, draw it on paper first, and make sure you can get the materials for any curves or odd angles. Then use surveyor's stakes to visualize the project in the desired location, and check for obstacles that might create problems through the growing season.

VERTICAL STRUCTURES

Quite a few plants will grow vertically. Corn does not need to be propped up, but other plants, including beans, cucumbers, peas, and tomatoes, do. Support these plants with cages or trellises, which are readily available from most nurseries.

Cages

I use so-called tomato cages for many plants, including cucumbers, eggplant, and peppers, as well as for tomatoes. These cages are usually cylindrically shaped wire structures. You grow your plants within them.

Trellises

To build a raised bed for peas or beans (which you will be planting in a row), make your bed narrow and long following the steps described earlier (see pages 18–19). A good size is 2 feet wide by whatever length you need—6 feet, 10 feet, or longer.

Build your own trellis in the center of this bed with the same wood material you used to build the bed. Just fasten with screws one 2-by-4-inch 6-foot piece of pressure-treated lumber into each end of the bed at the midway point on the short sides. Then fasten a board to the top of each upright, and stretch and fasten a piece of cattle panel or chicken wire between the uprights and the board across the top for support. Use a staple gun to fasten the chicken wire to the boards and cable ties for the cattle panels. Plant a row of beans or peas on either side of the trellis, which they can be trained to climb.

Another option is to go into any nearby woods. Gather fallen limbs that are straight and 7 to 8 feet long. Gather three limbs together at one end (which will be the top). Weave a piece of twine in and out of the limbs, three or so times, then tie off the twine. Pull out the bottoms of the limbs to make a teepee of sorts and stand it up in the middle of the bed. This structure is a great support for beans and peas.

Melons, such as cantaloupe and watermelon, can be grown vertically, but they are heavy and require support. You need a heavy-duty trellis that can support their weight. Then you will need to build "slings" to hold the melons as they ripen. "Cantaloupes slip off the vine" is not only a saying; it is a fact. When a cantaloupe is ripe, lifting it up will make it detach from the vine. If melons grow vertically without proper support, they will fall to the ground when ripe.

VERTICAL GARDENING

Vertical gardening is using a trellis or other support to allow plants to climb vertically rather than grow horizontally along the ground. When compared with conventional gardening, vertical gardening offers multiple advantages. First, it provides greater sunlight and air circulation for your plants, improving their health and increasing their productivity. Second, it minimizes your plants' exposure to certain pests and rodents found on the ground. Third, it makes your plants easier to harvest. If you are not bending and stooping, you'll experience less wear and tear on your back and knees. Fourth, it allows you to grow more plants in a smaller area. If you let a tomato plant sprawl all over your garden bed, it will take up a lot of room. If you use cages, you can plant your tomatoes 3 feet apart and get a lot of harvesting in a comparatively small amount of space.

Take advantage of plants' vertical growth habits by creating a one-of-a-kind trellis to be the focal point of your garden.

COVERS

Put a cover on your raised-bed gardens to speed soil warming in the spring and to retain soil warmth in the fall. A cover will protect your plants from damaging frost, giving you a head start on planting and extending your harvest season.

Garden Row Covers

Let's say you are in a hurry to get your garden planted in spring. If you must plant before the last frost, place garden row covers over your plants. These hoops covered with slitted or perforated polyethylene are meant to stay on only 3 to 4 weeks. They provide ventilation while retaining heat.

If you are really pushing your time line, I recommend planting your seedlings in black plastic garden mulch and then placing your row cover. Like the row cover, the mulch will help heat your soil. You can plant up to 3 weeks early with this method, but I would not use it for extremely sensitive plants, such as basil, cucumbers, or tomatoes. You are better off waiting until the right temperature for heat-loving crops.

Row covers will extend your harvest by a couple of weeks in fall.

Frost Protection

Frost protection covers are constructed of a woven, breathable fabric and can be left on your garden longer than row covers, because they will not overheat your plants. Frost protection covers come in a range of thicknesses that will increase the air temperature beneath them from 4 to 10 degrees

Fahrenheit. These covers are relatively lightweight, so you'll need to weigh down their edges to keep them secure.

Cloches

Cloches are like mini greenhouses. They typically are placed over an individual plant. At one time, cloches were glass, but now they are usually plastic. You may need to remove them during the day if they get too hot. Alternatively, you can prop up one side of your cloches so hot air can escape. Cloches work best if checked daily.

Cold Frames

Cold frames come in many configurations and are a great tool for extending your growing season. Recycle windows to build cold frames, or buy a kit. Cold frames are basically a frame with lids that can be propped up or removed. They are built to cover your entire raised bed. I always grow a little something in my cold frames in the winter—usually beets, brassicas, carrots, cilantro, and radishes.

CHAPTER THREE

SOIL

Soil quality is as important to the quality of your raised-bed garden as sunlight and water. Soil that does not have the nutrients your plants need or that is too acidic or too alkaline will yield poor results. Soil drainage and density will also affect your results.

In this chapter, you will determine how much soil you need, what type is best, and where to get it as well as how to have your soil tested and how to interpret the findings.

QUALITY

One of the great features of raised-bed gardening is that you don't have to rely on your yard soil—you can fill your beds with a soil that meets your plants' temperature, water retention, mineral, nutrient, and other needs.

Soil doesn't just hold plant roots in place. It insulates them, keeping them at a relatively constant temperature during extreme weather conditions. Plants do not like sudden temperature changes.

Soil supplies water to plants. Water is an essential part of photosynthesis, the process by which plants feed themselves or create energy. Without photosynthesis, plants will die.

Soil provides minerals. You may have seen products marked "NPK," for nitrogen, phosphorus, and potassium, some of the most essential nutrients in gardening. Nitrogen promotes growth and leaf greening. Phosphorus allows plants to flower and fruit. Proper potassium levels lead to healthy roots, which help fight disease.

Soil also provides nutrients—a consideration in plant pairing (see pages 10–11) and rotation (see pages 12–13). Topsoil—the top 2 to 8 inches of soil—contains the highest concentration of organic matter and nutrients, and, as you will learn in this chapter, it is the most desirable soil for raised beds (see page 30).

An important soil quality consideration is soil pH. On the pH scale of 0 to 14, a pH of 7 is neutral. Any pH below 7 is acidic, and any pH above 7 is base, or alkaline. A good pH range for most garden vegetables is 6.1 to 6.9 (see page 33 for how to measure pH). Some plants require more acidic soil, but they are not popular garden vegetables.

Another important soil quality consideration is soil density. Clay-filled soil is too compact for the roots of most flowers and vegetables to penetrate. Sandy soil is also not a good choice. It will not hold water. Most plants like fluffy soil that drains well.

To calculate how much soil you will need for your raised bed, use the example from chapter 2 for a 4-by-4-foot-by-6-inch bed.

Multiply the bed's width, length, and height in inches: 48 x 48 x 6 = 13,824.

If you want to know how many *cubic feet* of soil you need,

divide the product above by 1,728 (number of cubic inches in a cubic foot): 13,824 ÷ 1,728 = 8.

If you want to know how many *cubic yards* of soil you need,

divide the product by 46,656 (number of cubic inches in a cubic yard): 13,824 ÷ 46,656 = 0.29.

So, for our example, you need 8 cubic feet or 0.29 cubic yards of soil.

MIX

If you are on a tight budget, you can use topsoil from your yard, with the grass removed. Strain the soil through a screen and mix in compost equal to 25 percent of the topsoil. I do not recommend using your own yard's topsoil unless you have a budgetary issue. You will achieve better results with topsoil from a garden center or soil supplier.

Many nurseries sell a mix of topsoil and mulch by the truckload or the tractor bucket full. Nurseries typically sell the mixture they use for their own plants, so look around. If everything looks healthy, you will know you are getting a good mix. Discuss your needs with the nursery staff, who will be able to make recommendations.

To fill a small bed, you can purchase compost and topsoil in separate bags. Combine the contents on a tarp before transferring them to your bed. Don't combine the compost and topsoil in the bed. Doing so won't result in a good mix, and it might require you to step into the bed, which would compact the soil.

Seasoned gardeners develop their own combinations of peat moss, pumice, vermiculite, compost, sand, shredded bark, cow manure, lime, fertilizer, and so on. I caution novice gardeners against creating their own soil combinations. The results could be far from ideal, adversely affecting plants.

If you really want to try a homemade soil mixture, use this foolproof formula: Combine equal parts peat moss, vermiculite, and compost in a clean trash can (so you have a container to store any excess).

MAINTENANCE

You cannot fill your bed with soil once and forget it. Soil maintenance is an ongoing process. Your garden should always be kept clean. Any debris, such as dead leaves or overripe vegetables, should be removed to discourage disease and pests. Check for wilting, brown edges, holes in the leaves, and yellowing of your plants—all signs of a problem. Check under the leaves for bugs. If you find any, remove and dispose of them. If they are too small to remove, identify them and use an insecticidal soap. If you are unable to identify the bugs on your own, ask for help from your local extension agent (see Resources, page 125, for information on how to find an agent near you).

You should also start a compost pile or find a good local compost source, then add compost to your garden every fall or early spring.

Overfilling your bed will cause some soil to run out on rainy days. Depressions in the soil surface will end up holding water. Check for problems on a regular basis and always after a heavy rain. You may need to level the soil surface, especially after plantings.

When filling your bed, mound the soil slightly so it forms a shallow slope to the bed's sides. Because the dirt will settle, you will occasionally need to add more of it to your bed. Be especially sure to check your soil surface between seasons. Maintenance is easier when a bed is not planted.

Check the pH of your soil by purchasing a soil pH meter, available at nurseries, big box stores, and online retailers for $10 to $30. The meter will tell you whether your soil is too acidic or alkaline. Most pH meters include a manual with information on identifying and correcting problems.

A soil moisture meter alerts you to overwatering. It can be found at nurseries, big box stores, and online retailers, and it costs $10 to $30. If you can't find a moisture meter, stick your finger into the soil about 2 inches deep. If it is dry to that point, you should water more. If it is soggy, you are overwatering.

Kits for testing your soil's NPK (nitrogen, potassium, and phosphorus) cost about $25 and let you know if you need to add fertilizer. Look for these kits at nurseries, big box stores, and online retailers. If your plants are healthy, and you are happy with them, you may never need to use one of these kits. But it never hurts to know exactly what is going on in your garden. You may identify one change that makes a big improvement.

Other maintenance tasks are weeding; staking or trellising plants that require it; and adding mulch, such as straw or bark chips, to your garden to help retain moisture around your plants and deter weeds.

A garden is truly a work of joy. Most gardeners find that going out every day and doing a quick once-over is not a chore, but rather the most enjoyable time of the day—especially if they find something to pick and eat!

HOW TO TEST YOUR SOIL

Testing your soil is a good idea for first-time gardeners. It's the only way to know your soil's makeup. Is it too acidic or too alkaline? Does it have enough nitrogen, phosphorus, and potassium?

The best and easiest time to amend the soil is before you plant your garden. But because your garden is always changing, regularly testing and amending it is never a bad idea.

Aside from those kits that test soil moisture, pH, and NPK levels, the easiest and least expensive way to learn about your soil is to contact your local extension office (see page 125). Tell the agent the crops you are going to plant and request a soil testing. (My last soil testing cost about $15.) You will be given instructions on how to collect and mail a soil sample. Within a couple of weeks, you should receive a report identifying soil deficiencies and needed changes as well as instructions for making those changes.

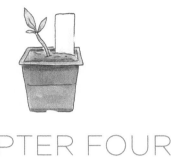

CHAPTER FOUR

PLANTING

Congratulations! You've identified where you'll place your raised-bed garden and determined its dimensions and configuration. You know what materials to use. You also know how to prepare the area and your soil.

Now you are getting to the best part. In this chapter, you will learn how to start your own seedlings and weigh the advantages and disadvantages of starting with seeds or seedlings. You will also learn where and how far apart to space your seeds or seedlings. Let's get growing.

SPACING

Following proper spacing guidelines is important when planting your seeds or plants. You will find this information on the seed packet or on the stake that comes with the seedling. Proper spacing ensures your plants have adequate room to grow, along with sufficient light and air circulation.

Vining plants, such as cucumbers, pole beans, and tomatoes, need a trellis or a cage. Be sure to leave room for these structures. If you have your tomato plants stacked too tightly, you'll have trouble harvesting all their fruit.

If you plant your seeds or seedlings too close to one another, they will compete for water, nutrients, and sunlight. The seeds or seedlings may seem far apart when you are planting them, but they will grow into some mighty big plants.

Seed packets and catalogs will provide information regarding seed planting, including depth and spacing requirements. Many packets will give you directions for starting non-direct-sow crop seeds indoors. They will also specify days to germination (sprouting), days to maturity (harvest time), and the height of the plant. That's a lot of information on one little seed

packet. If you are buying seedlings from a nursery, the information should be on the tag inserted in the pot.

Raised-bed gardens can be planted in rows or blocks, no matter the shape of the bed. When I plant in rows, I use my 4-foot-wide beds and plant my seeds about 1 foot in on either side. I use this method for plants such as basil, beans, cucumbers, peas, peppers, sunflowers, tomatoes, and zucchini. I also use rows for melons, but I plant only one row in a 4-foot bed, because melons need a lot of room to grow.

Compared with planting in rows, planting in blocks allows you to fit more plants in the same area. Let's use radishes, which should be spaced 3 inches apart, as an example. You plant the first seed and then others 3 inches to the right, left, front, and back of it. Keep going in this manner, planting every 3 inches in each direction. If you plant your entire 4-by-4-foot bed in this manner, you will end up with about 192 plants. When doing such intensive planting, keep in mind that all the plants will be ready to pick at the same time. It would be difficult for most people to eat 192 radishes within a week. The block planting approach is great, though, for crops you are going to preserve, such as by canning or dehydrating. Plants that work well for this type of planting are beets, carrots, chives, cilantro, onions, parsnips, and spinach.

For corn, I use a combination of the two methods, spacing each plant 4 inches apart. The rows should be 12 to 18 inches apart. So, in a 4-foot bed, I make four rows across (12 inches apart) and space the corn 4 inches apart in the rows.

Concentrate on quality instead of quantity. Always follow the recommended spacing.

SEED STARTING

Seed starting is not a requirement, but it offers many benefits. It allows you to experiment with varieties not carried by your local nursery and to control chemical inputs and growing practices. In addition, seed starting makes for a great family project—kids love to watch the progress of seedlings.

One other benefit: Seed starting gives plants with long growing seasons—and impatient gardeners—a head start. In many areas of the United

States, starting tomato seeds indoors is necessary to ensure that the plants have time to bear fruit before cold weather rolls back around.

Start your seeds indoors 6 to 8 weeks before the last frost in your area, then plant the seedlings outdoors in the garden after the danger of frost has passed.

To start seedlings first gather your tools and supplies. You will need:

- Plastic oil pan or bucket
- A good seed starting soil mix (a light and fluffy mix clearly marked for starting seeds)
- Peat pots
- Tray for the pots
- Seeds of choice
- Permanent marker
- Stakes to label the plants

- Vented lid (optional)
- Propagation mat (a heating pad for your plants)
- Adjustable fluorescent lights on a timer
- Liquid 20/20/20 houseplant fertilizer (a balanced blend of nitrogen, phosphorous, and potassium)

1. Add enough soil to the oil pan to fill your peat pots, then add water to make the soil just moist enough to be crumbly when pressed in your hand. No water should come out when you squeeze the soil.

2. Fill your peat pots with the moistened (not wet) soil, then place your pots in the tray. (I recommend peat pots, because they are biodegradable, can be planted directly in your garden, and allow healthy root growth. When planting time comes, pull the bottom off the pot and plant your seedling.)

3. Make a hole in the soil using the tip of your finger. Plant 2 or 3 seeds in each hole to the depth specified on the seed packet. Lightly cover each hole with the soil.

4. Mark your seeds with labels as you go, especially if you are planting two or more varieties of the same plant.

5. Place a vented lid over the tray. Keep the vent open until the seedlings appear, then remove the lid. This (and only this) step is optional. Some people cover their trays with plastic wrap or use a spray bottle to keep the soil moist.

6. Place the tray on a propagation mat and plug it in. The mat will raise the soil temperature to assist germination. You can put the tray on the top of your refrigerator, which is warm, but I prefer to keep mine at eye level so I can regularly monitor the seedlings' progress.

7. Once the seedlings sprout, place fluorescent lights directly above the tray, as close as 2 to 4 inches away from the seedling tops. Raise the lights as the plants grow. (Without sufficient light, your plants will become yellow and spindly.)

8. The first "leaves" to appear are the cotyledons; they are actually part of the seed. When the first set of true leaves appears, start fertilizing. (If your soil mix contains fertilizer, skip this step.) Use about a quarter of the amount of fertilizer recommended on the fertilizer bag label, but before you apply the fertilizer, dilute it—and make it half the strength specified on the label.

TRUE LEAVES

EP COTYL

COTYLEDONS

Many seeds, if stored in a cool, dry, and dark place, could be viable for as many as 5 years, but some seeds are viable for shorter or longer times. Before you plant seeds of suspect viability, do a germination test to determine whether they will sprout. Place 10 seeds on a paper towel that is damp but not dripping wet. Roll up the towel and place it in a resealable storage bag. Partially seal the bag and place it in a cool, dry place such as in a drawer or cupboard.

In 2 or 3 days, check to see how many seeds have sprouted. Moldy seeds do *not* count as sprouted. Discard both the moldy seeds and any seeds that have germinated. Continue to check the seeds daily for up to 2 weeks, if necessary. When you are checking the seeds, moisten the paper towel, if needed.

Discontinue the test early if all seeds have been counted.

Calculate your germination rate. If, at the end of 2 weeks, 4 of 10 seeds have sprouted, you have a 40 percent germination rate (5 seeds is equal to a 50 percent rate; 6 seeds, a 60 percent rate; and so on). Most commercial seed companies aim for a 90 to 95 percent germination rate. If your rate was lower and you still want to use your seeds, add extra seeds to each hole to account for the germination rate suggested by your test.

PLANTING

Let's get planting. Gather all your seeds, seedlings, and tools. Make sure you have a water source nearby, because you will be watering immediately after you plant. I recommend having a ruler, a couple of stakes, some twine to run between the stakes, and a garden trowel. If you are going to put cages on any of the seedlings, have them handy as well.

The best time of day to plant seedlings is in the evening when relative cool will give your plants the best opportunity to recover from transplanting and become acclimated.

Unlike seedlings, seeds can be planted any time during the day.

Planting Seeds

Seeds will be planted in a row or in a block (see pages 44-45). Let's use green beans—either bush or pole beans—as an example. Pole beans need to be trained to climb a trellis or some kind of support, so supply that support as soon as your plants start to grow (see page 21).

SEEDS VERSUS SEEDLINGS

Seedlings are seeds that have sprouted, essentially young plants. Typically, seedlings are started 6 to 8 weeks before you are ready to plant them outdoors, in both spring and fall.

Always purchase seeds from reputable seed companies to be confident they are fresh and have been handled properly. Any leftover seeds can be stored for the next year in a sealed plastic bag that you'll put in your refrigerator (it is cool and dark). Insert a desiccant (like the silica packet you get in new shoes, vitamins, or some electronics) in the bag to keep the seeds dry. Seed life varies from 1 to 5 years, depending on the type of seed, its quality, and how it was handled before you received it. When using older seeds, plant 2 or 3 in each hole, because their germination rate (the number that sprout) will be lower than that of newer seeds.

Plants with a relatively long growth cycle do better when planted as seedlings. In some areas, the growing season is just not long enough for those plants to mature and ripen. Moreover, in some areas the soil is not warm enough in spring to accommodate a full growing cycle. Seeds require a certain soil temperature before they will germinate or sprout. This temperature varies with each type of seed.

Some plants do not like to be transplanted and therefore are best planted directly into the ground as seeds. (See chapter 6, Plant Profiles, for more information.) A few examples of seeds that should be directly sown into the garden are carrots, corn, lettuce, peas, and radishes. Check your seed packet for planting directions.

Any garden plant you see in nurseries every spring will be agreeable to transplanting, including egg-plant, peppers, and tomatoes.

To plant seeds in a row:

1. Place a stake at each end of the row and tie a piece of twine between them to mark your row.

2. Use a trowel to make a row or furrow to the depth specified on the seed packet.

3. Place a tape measure along the side of the row. Use it to properly space your seeds according to the seed packet's instructions. Plant the entire row.

4. Remove your tape measure and the row markers. Lightly cover the soil by pushing the dirt back over the seeds with the trowel.

1. Outline the block with a shallow furrow or trench.

2. Lay your tape measure along the side to properly space your seeds. Let's say you are planting radishes 3 inches apart, to the depth indicated on the seed packet. Start at the front and work your way back, row by row.

3. Start at 3 inches, 6 inches, and so on in the first row.

4. Move your tape measure back 3 inches and plant the next section. Keep going until your block is full.

5. Cover the seeds with soil.

Planting Seedlings

Plants purchased as seedlings tend to be plants that should be planted in rows. Exceptions may exist, but I can't think of any. To plant seedlings, use the method described for planting seeds in a row.

If you started your own seedlings, they should be in biodegradable peat pots. If you have purchased them, they might be in peat or plastic pots.

1. If the seedlings are in peat pots, simply remove the bottoms of the pots—just tear them off. You can throw them in the holes you prepare for the seedlings.

2. If the seedlings are in plastic pots, remove them and all the dirt.

3. Plant your seedlings at the depth they were planted in the pots. The only exception to this rule of thumb is tomato seedlings. Remove the bottom 2 or 3 sets of leaves from their stems and gently bend the stems. Roots will grow off this part of the stem. Make sure that the de-leafed and bent part of the stems are under the ground.

Final Steps

Place any cages (see page 21) needed over young seedlings at this time.

> **TIP:** I always wrap several layers of plastic wrap around the bottoms of my tomato cages (about 12 inches high) to protect the seedlings from harsh spring winds.

Don't forget to water all your seeds and seedlings. Do a deep watering, letting the water soak down into the ground to reach the roots of your seedlings. Avoid getting water on the leaves. You will learn more about watering in the next chapter.

CHAPTER FIVE

GROWING AND HARVESTING

If you keep up with your garden maintenance, you will find that it takes just a little time daily. You can do many of the chores while you are out visiting your garden in the evening. If you let chores like weeding slide, they will quickly become chores you don't enjoy. This chapter covers plant care basics.

WATERING

Watering baffles many beginner gardeners. How much is too much water? How much is too little? Overwatered plants may appear limp or soggy, a condition you might mistakenly attribute to underwatering and attempt to remedy by adding more water. The best way to test whether water is needed is to put your finger into the soil. If the soil is wet at about 1 inch down, the plant does not need water. If it is dry at about 2 inches down, give your plant a drink.

Most plants need 1 to 2 inches of water per week. If you are in a rainy area, get a rain gauge. If you get 1 inch of rain every week and your soil is damp 1 inch down, your plants will not need to be watered as much as those in a dry area. Unless you are in an extreme drought condition, it is best to underwater rather than overwater.

Watering is best done in early morning, before the sun is high in the sky. Because this time of day is cooler, the water will soak into the ground rather than evaporate into the air. Your objective is a deep, regular watering, reaching the roots of the plants. Drip irrigation or a soaker hose will yield the best results.

Sprinklers are not recommended (especially at night). They have a tendency to water leaves and scatter water on top of the soil rather than give your plants a deep drink. Watering at night can lead to root rot and fungal diseases of the plant stem, especially if you are getting water on the leaves.

Never water a limp plant during the heat of the day. Wait until evening to determine whether water is needed by putting your finger 1 inch in the soil near the plant. If the soil is dry, water the plant.

Keeping the soil light and fluffy will help the water get to plant roots, where it is needed. Use a hand cultivator to work the dirt up around your plant, being careful to avoid the roots. To conserve moisture, add mulch to your garden once your plants start producing. The objective is to get the plants to put out more roots searching for water. When plants are watered every day, they do not search for water. The result is a shallow root system and a weak plant. Instead, do a deep watering every couple of days to encourage strong roots.

MAINTENANCE

You have the garden all set to go. Now you just need to do some maintenance as you work toward the best possible garden.

Thinning

The directions on your seed packets describe how to thin seedlings—that is, achieve the optimal distance between mature plants. Thinning can be tough love: Pull out the plants that are too close together as soon as possible to give the remaining plants the best opportunity to become healthy. Overcrowding is not good for the garden.

Mulching

Mulch doesn't just help maintain a constant temperature for plant root systems. It helps decrease weeds and increase soil moisture. Keep 4 inches of shredded leaves or straw around your plants.

Fertilizing

Plants require varying amounts and types of fertilizer. Test your soil before applying any specific fertilizer (see page 33).

To feed my entire garden, I use a good general-purpose plant food, such as Miracle-Gro, that can be found at most nurseries and big box stores. I mix it with water and apply it every 2 weeks when the garden is producing.

Weeding

Weeding is not such a big chore if done on a regular basis. When you wander around your garden each evening, reach down and pull tiny weeds as they appear. The biggest problem with weeding is saying, "Oh, I'll just wait until the weekend and do all the weeding at once." That's a mistake. Once the weeds get ahead of you, it can feel impossible to catch up with them. Mulching will help keep weeds at bay.

Bug Inspection

Bug inspection is like weeding. Bugs will get out of control if you don't deal with them the minute you see them. I just reach out and pluck them off the plant. If you have a big infestation, use one of the natural soap-based horticultural soaps readily available at most garden supply stores to deal with the problem. I prefer not to use chemical pesticides in my garden.

Harvesting

Harvesting is another task not to put off. Once a veggie is ready to be picked, harvest it and enjoy it. If you leave vegetables on the plant to rot, they will encourage disease and also slow the production of the plant they are on.

Maintaining Your Plants

Herbs, such as basil, will flower when mature. To get a bushier, more compact plant, you should pinch off these flowers. Always remove any dead leaves or branches, which become an open invitation for pests and disease.

Tomato plants have suckers—new shoots that form from a branch off the main stem. They produce no tomatoes and compete with the rest of the plant for nutrients. Pinch them off to produce larger tomatoes and a higher yield.

HARVESTING

Harvest time is usually busy, especially if you have planted enough food to preserve, can, dehydrate, or otherwise keep for future use. If you have planted just enough food to eat fresh, harvest season will be more manageable. But, keep in mind, once a garden starts producing, it keeps on producing. What a great time of year!

Open up your garden journal. You noted when you planted your seeds and seedlings, and you estimated the number of days to harvest, which should help you determine when harvesting will start.

During this season, check your garden daily for any issues and ready-to-pick produce. You don't want to miss out on the bounty of your effort, and as you learned, leaving crops on the plant is an invitation for bugs and disease.

The best time to harvest is morning, when it is not too warm for you or the plants. But I must confess, I walk through the garden at lunch and dinnertime to harvest a couple of items to eat. Nothing beats freshly picked produce that you grew.

Chapter 6 has specific information about harvesting each common garden plant, but here is some general guidance to get you started.

Herbs and Leafy Greens

Herbs are one of the easiest plants to harvest. Once they have green leaves, pick them as desired. If you prefer a large bunch of herbs, let them keep growing, then use scissors to cut them back to within 2 inches of the ground. They will grow back.

Lettuce, spinach, and other greens are harvested in the same manner as herbs.

Corn

Corn is ready to harvest when the silk turns brown and you can feel kernels all the way down the ear. Pull the husk back a little at the top if you are not completely sure. Twist and pull each ear with a jerking motion.

Tomatoes

First, know which colors of tomato you are growing. I can't tell you how many green zebra tomatoes have been overlooked in my garden because they never turn red. You can leave tomatoes to ripen fully on the vine, but you run the risk of letting them overripen. I like to pick mine when they have a blush of color, then let them ripen on the counter in a cool, dry spot. Never put a fresh-picked tomato in the refrigerator—it will not ripen.

You can pick red varieties when they are full size but still green, and fry them. To pick a tomato, get a firm grip on it and pull. Be careful not to squash the tomato.

Cantaloupes

As you learned, cantaloupes should literally slip off the vine. You can also smell them. If they smell like melons, they are ripe.

Watermelons

Watermelons are ripe when the tendril closest to the fruit turns brown. The tendril is a curly shaped part of the stem that looks almost like a pig's tail. It is used by vining plants for support.

WEEDS

I don't know any gardener who likes weeds. They compete with your vegetable plants for nutrients and water. Put up all the WEED-FREE ZONE signs you want. The weeds will continue to ignore you and grow if you let them.

Weeding is easier in the morning, when the ground is still damp from the dew or your watering. If the ground is dry, add a little water to soften it. Discourage weeds and disrupt their establishment by regularly breaking up the ground with a garden cultivator (see page 50). Pick small weeds by tugging on them as close to their roots as possible. Try to get all the roots. (Get a kneeling bench for weeding so at least your knees will be comfortable.)

Mulching, as you learned on page 51, helps minimize weeds by keeping sunlight away from them so it is harder for them to grow. Inevitably, some will get through even the densest mulch and must be picked by hand.

Plastic garden mulch has been my favorite method for keeping weeds out. Lay this polyethylene film over the garden bed to erect a physical barrier for the weeds. Then punch holes in the film to make room to plant your seeds and seedlings.

Plastic garden mulch comes in black, red, blue, white on black, and several other colors, and it needs to be used with a drip irrigation system underneath it; otherwise, water will not go through the cover. Its benefits are fewer weeds, better water retention, less water required in general, increased soil temperature, and better retention of nutrients in the soil (nutrients won't leach away with excessive rains).

To minimize establishment of weeds between your final harvest and your next growing season, cover your garden with a thick layer of newspaper, cardboard, or plastic mulch.

COMMON PROBLEMS

Pests or disease can occur in even the best maintained garden. If you can determine the cause of the issue, you can probably resolve it. Here are a few problems that gardeners may encounter.

Pests

If you see a bug in your garden, do not panic. Not all bugs are detrimental to your plants. Look for any plant damage or distress before you attempt to get rid of every bug you see. If your plants look healthy, continue to monitor the situation.

Pests manifest themselves in several ways. You may see holes in the leaves or bug droppings. Or, you may notice the plant wilt and, ultimately, die. If you are unable to identify a pest, ask your local extension agent for help (see page 125) with identification and eradication.

Disease

Many diseases harm specific plants and can be caused by mold, virus, fungus, or bacteria. Signs of disease include curled, wilting leaves, leaves with a mosaic pattern, or leaves or stems with spots.

You may need to use insecticidal soaps, erect row covers, remove affected plants, or grow a disease-resistant variety. Again, an extension agent can help you identify the issue.

Environmental Issues

Blossom end rot in tomatoes, squash, and peppers is caused by a lack of calcium in the soil and irregular watering. It will show up as a brown spot at the bottom of the vegetable and will normally clear up on its own as the season progresses. Cut out the spot and eat the rest of the vegetable.

You may have plants that bolt, or flower, too early because of warmer temperatures. This issue can be solved by planting bolt-resistant varieties, which seed catalogs will identify for you.

Check your pH and NPK levels (see pages 31-33) if you see stunted growth, yellowing leaves, or brown spots on leaves, or if no vegetables are reaching the harvest state. You may have overfertilized.

Animals

Deer, raccoons, mice, and other animals can be managed with fencing, netting, or floating row covers.

CHAPTER SIX

PLANT PROFILES

This chapter covers some of the most popular garden plants. You will learn the specifics of each one, such as when to plant it, whether to plant it as a seed or a seedling, how many days until it can be harvested, and when it can be planted outdoors. You will learn about the location and specific needs of each plant, as well as find growing tips. You will learn when and how to harvest the plant and how to spot problems that it may encounter.

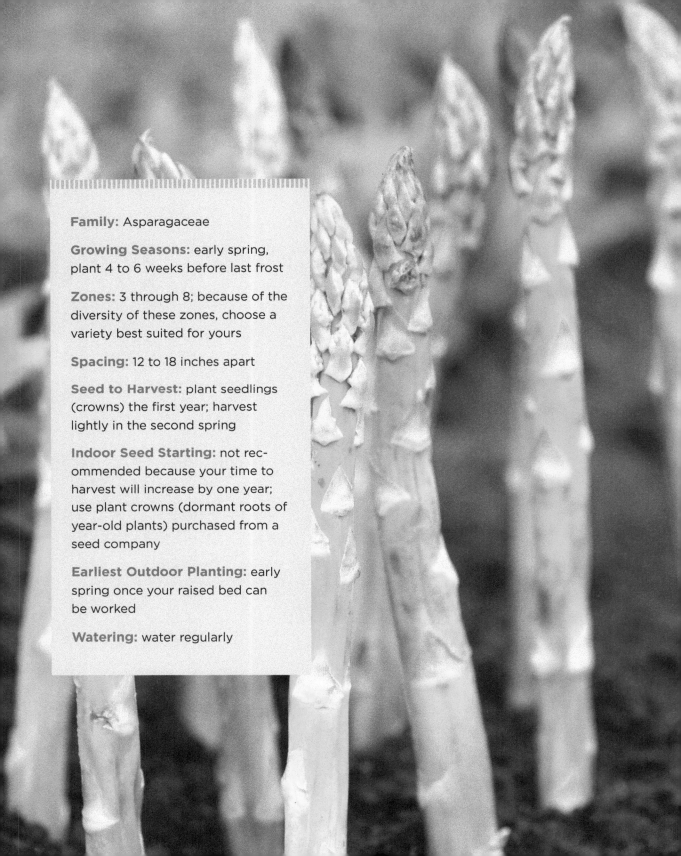

Family: Asparagaceae

Growing Seasons: early spring, plant 4 to 6 weeks before last frost

Zones: 3 through 8; because of the diversity of these zones, choose a variety best suited for yours

Spacing: 12 to 18 inches apart

Seed to Harvest: plant seedlings (crowns) the first year; harvest lightly in the second spring

Indoor Seed Starting: not recommended because your time to harvest will increase by one year; use plant crowns (dormant roots of year-old plants) purchased from a seed company

Earliest Outdoor Planting: early spring once your raised bed can be worked

Watering: water regularly

ASPARAGUS

Asparagus officinalis

Asparagus does not like to compete with weeds, so maintain your bed well. Asparagus plants can live 15 or more years, producing every year once they are established.

Starting

Location: full sun, part shade

Transplanting: Plant crowns in a trench 8 inches deep. Spread the roots and cover them with 1 to 2 inches of soil. You will add soil to the trench as the plants grow.

Planting: Add lime and fertilizer before planting crowns. Asparagus likes a pH near 7.

Growing

Keep asparagus watered in the first year, especially during times without rain. Do not overwater. The roots do not like to be overly wet. Mulch heavily to minimize weeds.

Harvesting

Harvest the spears before the tops develop fern-like leaves. Cut at ground level.

Problems

Asparagus beetle: Remove manually.

Fusarium wilt: Use fungicide.

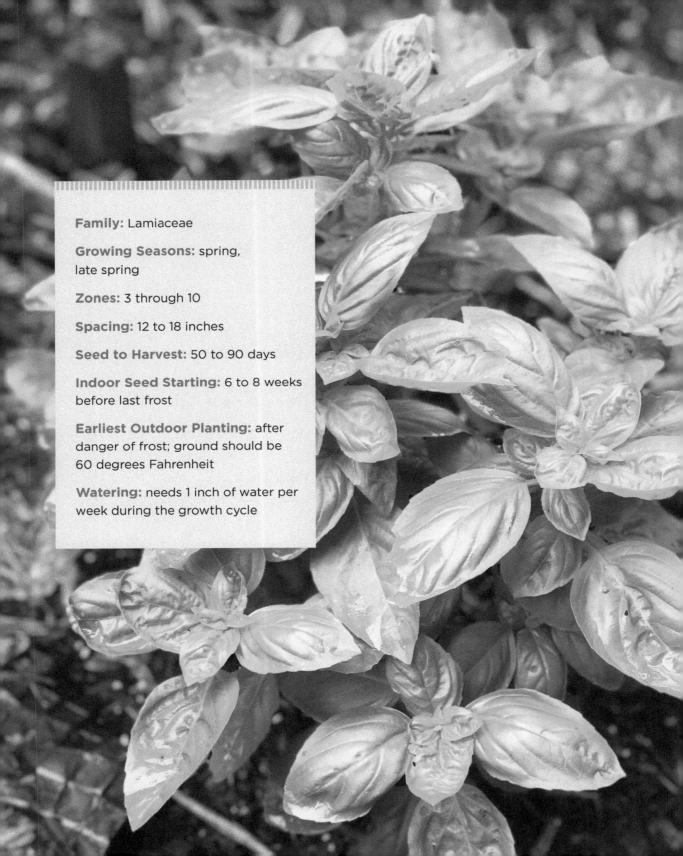

Family: Lamiaceae

Growing Seasons: spring, late spring

Zones: 3 through 10

Spacing: 12 to 18 inches

Seed to Harvest: 50 to 90 days

Indoor Seed Starting: 6 to 8 weeks before last frost

Earliest Outdoor Planting: after danger of frost; ground should be 60 degrees Fahrenheit

Watering: needs 1 inch of water per week during the growth cycle

BASIL

Ocimum basilicum

Try growing the large-leaf basil for making wraps and purple basil for creating a focal spot in your garden.

Starting

Location: full sun

Planting: Cover seeds with ¼ inch of soil when planting directly in the garden.

Growing

Basil should not be allowed to dry out. Regular watering is best. To create bushy plants, pinch off the plant tops when they start to flower.

Harvesting

Pull off the leaves as desired.

Problems

If you are growing your basil in a warm area, pick varieties that are slow to bolt.

Family: Chenopodiaceae

Growing Seasons: early spring or late fall in warmer climates; late spring or early fall in colder climates

Zones: 3 through 10

Spacing: 12 inches apart

Seed to Harvest: 50 to 60 days

Indoor Seed Starting: not recommended

Earliest Outdoor Planting: in cooler climates, early spring once your raised bed can be worked; in frost-free areas, sow in the fall

Watering: 1 inch of water per week

BEET

Beta vulgaris

Beet greens and roots are edible. They can be roasted, pickled, grilled, or boiled, and they freeze well.

Starting

Location: full sun, part shade

Planting: Beets do not like acidic soil; they prefer a pH between 6 and 7.

Growing

Too much nitrogen will make the tops grow better than the roots.

Harvesting

Harvest beet greens when they are 4 to 5 inches long. Harvest the roots at 1 to 3 inches in diameter.

Problems

Leaf miner: Handpick and destroy affected leaves.

Leaf spot: Keep water off the green tops.

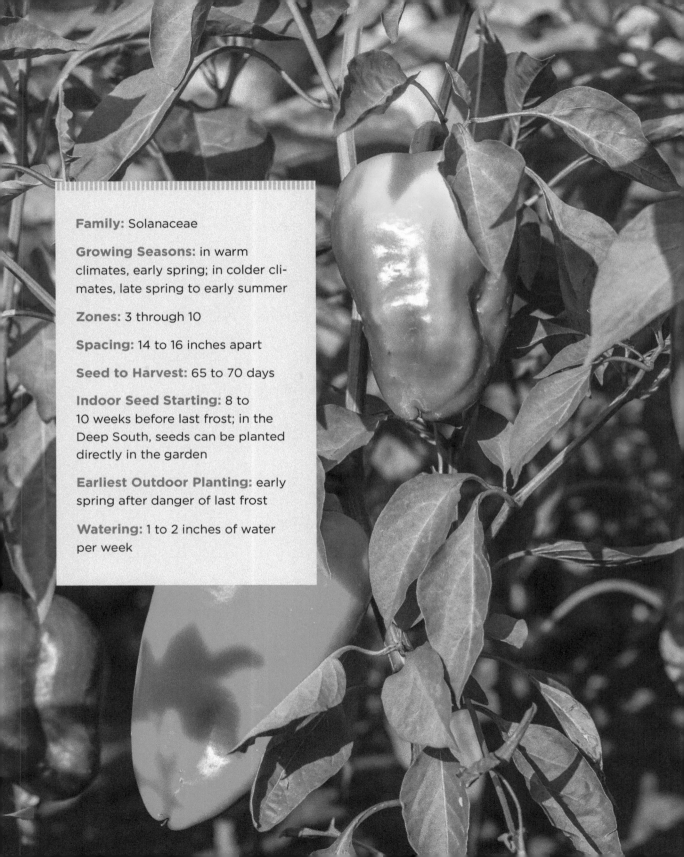

Family: Solanaceae

Growing Seasons: in warm climates, early spring; in colder climates, late spring to early summer

Zones: 3 through 10

Spacing: 14 to 16 inches apart

Seed to Harvest: 65 to 70 days

Indoor Seed Starting: 8 to 10 weeks before last frost; in the Deep South, seeds can be planted directly in the garden

Earliest Outdoor Planting: early spring after danger of last frost

Watering: 1 to 2 inches of water per week

BELL PEPPER

Capsicum annuum

Do not plant bell peppers where in the previous year you planted eggplant, peppers, potatoes, or tomatoes.

Starting

Location: full sun

Growing

Too much nitrogen will cause the plant to produce more leaves than peppers.

Harvesting

Cut peppers off the stem rather than pulling them off. Peppers develop more flavor as they mature.

Problems

Aphids: Use natural soap and water.

Blossom end rot: This condition normally clears up on its own. Cut out the affected portion and eat the rest of the pepper.

Cucumber mosaic virus: Pull and dispose of infected plants; choose a different planting location next year.

Family: Brassicaceae

Growing Seasons: spring, fall, cool weather

Zones: 3 through 10; if in a warmer climate, plant heat-tolerant seeds

Spacing: 18 to 24 inches in rows 3 feet apart

Seed to Harvest: 45 to 60 days

Indoor Seed Starting: 7 to 9 weeks before the last spring frost; give seedlings 14 to 16 hours of light using fluorescent lighting

Earliest Outdoor Planting: 2 weeks before the last spring frost; in fall, in warm climates, 85 to 100 days before the first frost

Watering: moderate and even; water only the roots, not the heads

BROCCOLI

Brassica oleracea var. italica

If you live in a warm climate, a fall planting is best, because broccoli thrives in cool weather.

Starting

Location: full sun, can tolerate some shade, but plants will grow more slowly

Planting: Broccoli prefers a temperature between 64 degrees and 73 degrees Fahrenheit. It can be sowed outdoors with soil temperatures as low as 40 degrees Fahrenheit.

Growing

Broccoli can tolerate frost. Because it has a shallow root system, the use of mulch, rather than a cultivator, is recommended.

Harvesting

If you see yellow flowers, harvest the heads and use them immediately, because they are slightly beyond their prime. Harvest the central head of each broccoli plant with a pair of garden shears to encourage growth on the side shoots, which will continue to grow heads for several weeks.

Problems

Aphids: Use an insecticidal soap or a heavy spray of water to remove them.

Cabbage worms: Remove them manually, or use row covers to keep them off.

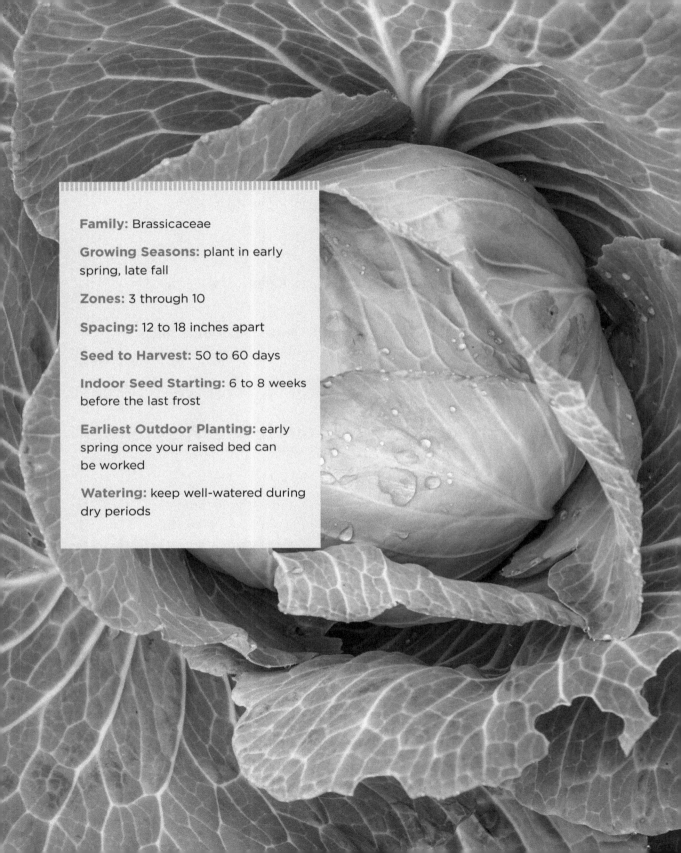

Family: Brassicaceae

Growing Seasons: plant in early spring, late fall

Zones: 3 through 10

Spacing: 12 to 18 inches apart

Seed to Harvest: 50 to 60 days

Indoor Seed Starting: 6 to 8 weeks before the last frost

Earliest Outdoor Planting: early spring once your raised bed can be worked

Watering: keep well-watered during dry periods

CABBAGE

Brassica oleracea var. capitata

Some varieties of cabbage grow flowers. The leaves of those plants are edible, but they are usually used as a garnish. Check your seed packets to verify you have edible cabbage leaves.

Starting

Location: full sun

Planting: Plants will withstand a light frost.

Growing

Cabbage has a shallow root system. Avoid damaging it when weeding or cultivating.

Harvesting

Harvest when the heads are firm.

Problems

Cabbage aphids: Use an insecticidal soap or a heavy spray of water to remove them.

Cabbage worms: Remove them manually or use row covers to keep them off.

Clubroot: Remove the affected plants.

Cutworms: Remove them manually.

Family: Cucurbitaceae

Growing Seasons: in warmer climates, early spring; in colder climates, late spring to early summer

Zones: 3 through 10

Spacing: 36 to 48 inches apart

Seed to Harvest: 70 to 85 days

Indoor Seed Starting: 3 to 4 weeks before planting, but direct sowing is recommended

Earliest Outdoor Planting: after danger of frost has passed

Watering: 1 to 2 inches of water per week

CANTALOUPE

Cucumis melo var. cantalupensis

Most people will grow their cantaloupes on the ground rather than on a trellis, because they "slip" off the vine when they are ripe.

Starting

Location: full sun

Growing

Melons have a shallow root system; avoid damaging it when weeding or cultivating.

If you are growing melons on the ground, use plenty of mulch so they do not sit in the soil.

Harvesting

Ripe melons will "slip" from the vine. You will not need to exert much pressure to get them to release.

Once they start to smell like a melon, they are ripe.

Problems

Aphids: Use an insecticidal soap or a heavy spray of water to remove them.

Powdery mildew: Spray plants with a solution of 2 to 3 tablespoons of white vinegar per gallon of water.

Squash bugs: Remove eggs from the underside of leaves in the morning and later in the day.

Wilt disease: Use a fungicide.

Family: Apiaceae

Growing Seasons: spring, fall, depending on location; check your zone for specific times

Zones: 3 through 10

Spacing: 3 to 4 inches apart in rows 1 to 2 feet apart

Seed to Harvest: 50 to 80 days

Indoor Seed Starting: plant directly in the garden because they do not like to be transplanted

Earliest Outdoor Planting: after danger of heavy frost; in frost-free areas plant in fall

Watering: keep moist but not saturated; best done by drip irrigation; do not water foliage

CARROT

Daucus carot

Plant carrots every couple of weeks for nonstop harvesting.

Starting

Location: full sun

Seeding: Do not start indoors. Plant direct.

Planting: Cover seeds with ½ inch of soil. Plant them in deep, loose soil so the roots can grow.

Growing

Only weeding and watering are needed. Carrots need 1 inch of water per week during the growth cycle. Do not try to grow them in clay soil.

Harvesting

Simply twist and pull the roots, being careful not to pull the tops off. Clean the carrots and cut the green tops to just above the root for storage.

Problems

Aster yellows disease: Spread by the aster leafhopper, this disease causes shortened tops and hairy roots. Control the pest and keep this disease away using a sticky trap found at hardware stores.

Fusarium: This fungus causes dry rot of the root when carrots stay in the ground past their prime. To prevent fusarium, pick carrots at maturity.

Family: Amaryllidaceae

Growing Seasons: spring, late spring

Zones: 3 through 10

Spacing: 3 to 4 inches apart

Seed to Harvest: 80 to 90 days

Indoor Seed Starting: 8 to 10 weeks before last spring frost

Earliest Outdoor Planting: after danger of heavy frost

Watering: water seedlings thoroughly after planting; plants need about 1 inch of water per week

CHIVES

Allium schoenoprasum

Chives are a great focal point in a garden bed and a welcome addition to many cuisines. For best production and healthiest plants, divide clumps every 3 to 4 years.

Starting

Location: full sun

Seeding: Seeds can be started indoors or directly sown in the soil.

Transplanting: Plant seedlings with plenty of room for the root ball.

Planting: In the garden, cover seeds with ¼ inch of soil.

Growing

Weeding and watering are the only maintenance needed.

Harvesting

Clip plants to 1 inch above the ground. The tops will regrow.

Problems

Chives usually remain pest-free.

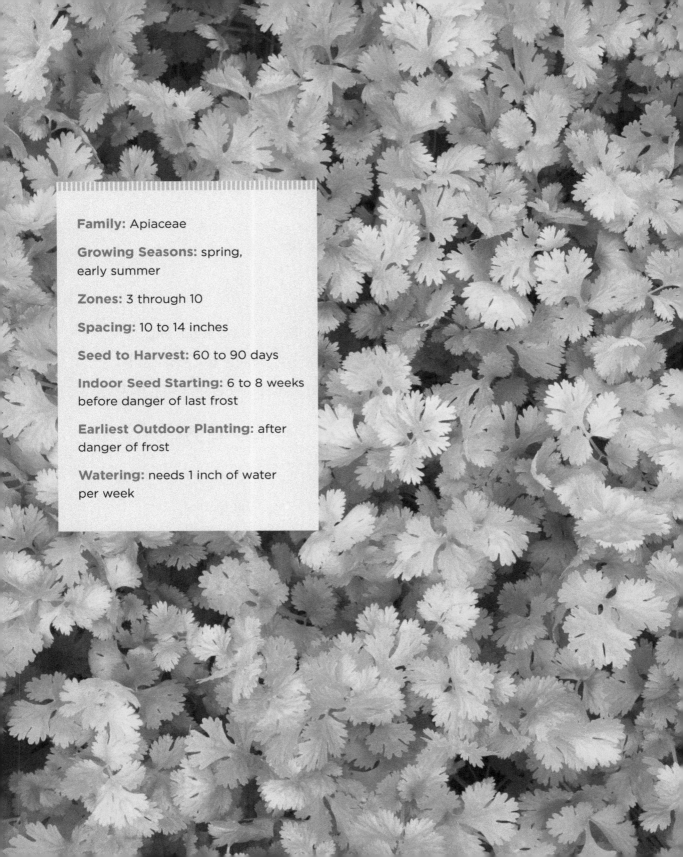

Family: Apiaceae

Growing Seasons: spring, early summer

Zones: 3 through 10

Spacing: 10 to 14 inches

Seed to Harvest: 60 to 90 days

Indoor Seed Starting: 6 to 8 weeks before danger of last frost

Earliest Outdoor Planting: after danger of frost

Watering: needs 1 inch of water per week

CILANTRO

Coriandrum sativum

Cilantro can be harvested as cilantro (the fresh herb) or coriander (the seed). For cilantro, harvest plants once green leaves are present, before the plants flower. For coriander, harvest the seeds once they turn grayish-brown.

Starting

Location: full sun

Seeding: Plant indoors 6 to 8 weeks before the last frost.

Planting: Cover seeds with ¼ inch of soil. Plant every 3 weeks if you want a continuous harvest.

Growing

Cilantro needs 1 inch of water per week. Do not fertilize.

Harvesting

Cut with scissors to 2 inches above the ground.

Problems

Keep soil moist so plants don't wilt.

Family: Poaceae

Growing Seasons: spring, late spring

Zones: 3 through 10

Spacing: 5 to 6 inches in rows 2 to 3 feet apart

Seed to Harvest: 70 to 85 days

Indoor Seed Starting: directly sow in the garden

Earliest Outdoor Planting: after danger of frost

Watering: needs 1 to 2 inches of water per week during the growth cycle; soaker hose or drip irrigation is best

CORN

Zea mays

Keep different varieties away from one another so they do not cross-pollinate, which could affect the flavor and quality of your harvested corn.

Starting

Location: full sun

Planting: Cover seeds with 1 inch of soil. Mix slow-release fertilizer into the soil when planting, according to the instructions on the label.

Growing

Weeding and watering are the only maintenance needed.

Harvesting

Each stalk usually produces two ears of corn, but hybrid varieties may have a higher yield. Harvest when the silk at the end of the ears is dry and brown and the ear feels plump. You may need to pull back the husk a little to see what you have. Give the ear a twist and a good tug to release it.

Problems

Corn earworms: These pests are found at the ends of the ears. Either trim and discard the ends, or do what I've done successfully for 20 worm-free years and squirt food-grade mineral oil into the ends of the ears when the silk turns brown.

Family: Cucurbitaceae, sometimes called curbits

Growing Seasons: soil temperature at least 60 degrees Fahrenheit

Zones: 3 through 10

Spacing: 18 to 36 inches apart; bush varieties can be planted closer together

Seed to Harvest: 50 to 70 days

Indoor Seed Starting: 3 to 4 weeks before the last frost, but direct sowing outdoors is recommended

Earliest Outdoor Planting: after the last frost

Watering: steady supply of water; drip irrigation on a timer is best

CUCUMBER

Cucumis sativus

Cucumber plants are prolific, so do not plant too many. Buy pickling cucumber seeds to make pickles and slicing cucumber seeds to eat fresh. Do not use slicing cucumbers to make pickles; they soften when pickled.

Starting

Location: full sun

Planting: Do not plant cucumbers until the soil reaches 60 degrees Fahrenheit.

Growing

Bush cucumbers do not need to be staked, but regular cucumber varieties do.

Harvesting

Cut rather than pull cucumbers off the vine. Do not leave overripe cucumbers on the vine, because the plant will take that as a signal to stop production.

Problems

Slugs and snails: Handpick and discard them.

Family: Fabaceae

Growing Seasons: early to late spring, depending on zone; check your zone for specific times

Zones: 3 through 10

Spacing: 2 to 4 inches apart

Seed to Harvest: 50 to 55 days

Indoor Seed Starting: not recommended

Earliest Outdoor Planting: early spring once the danger of frost has passed

Watering: 1 inch per week

GREEN BEANS

Phaseolus vulgaris

Beans are available as bush beans or pole beans. Bush beans do not need the support of a trellis, but pole beans do.

Starting

Location: full sun

Growing

When watering, do not wet the leaves. If they do get wet, do not handle them when wet because disease may result.

Harvesting

Beans are easy to pick right off the vine.

Problems

Aphids: Use an insecticidal soap or a heavy spray of water to remove them.

Bacterial blights: Use copper fungicide.

Spider mites: Use neem oil.

Family: Brassicaceae

Growing Seasons: spring, fall

Zones: 3 through 10

Spacing: 12 to 18 inches apart

Seed to Harvest: 50 to 55 days

Indoor Seed Starting: direct sow outdoors up to 3 months before the last expected frost

Earliest Outdoor Planting: early spring once your raised bed can be worked; will germinate as low as 45 degrees Fahrenheit

Watering: do not let the plants dry out during drought periods

KALE

Brassica oleracea var. acephala

Kale has many health benefits. It is good for digestion, high in iron and vitamin K, and filled with antioxidants. You can plant it from early spring to early summer, but if you plant it in late summer, you can harvest it from fall until the first ground freeze.

Starting

Location: full sun, part shade

Planting: Kale is easy to grow and prefers well-drained soil.

Growing

To reduce disease and pests, do not plant kale in the same location as other cole crops (cruciferous vegetables like broccoli or cabbage) for 3 to 4 years.

Harvesting

Kale harvested after a frost will have a sweeter flavor.

Pick the outer leaves and leave the center.

Problems

Kale is relatively pest- and disease-free.

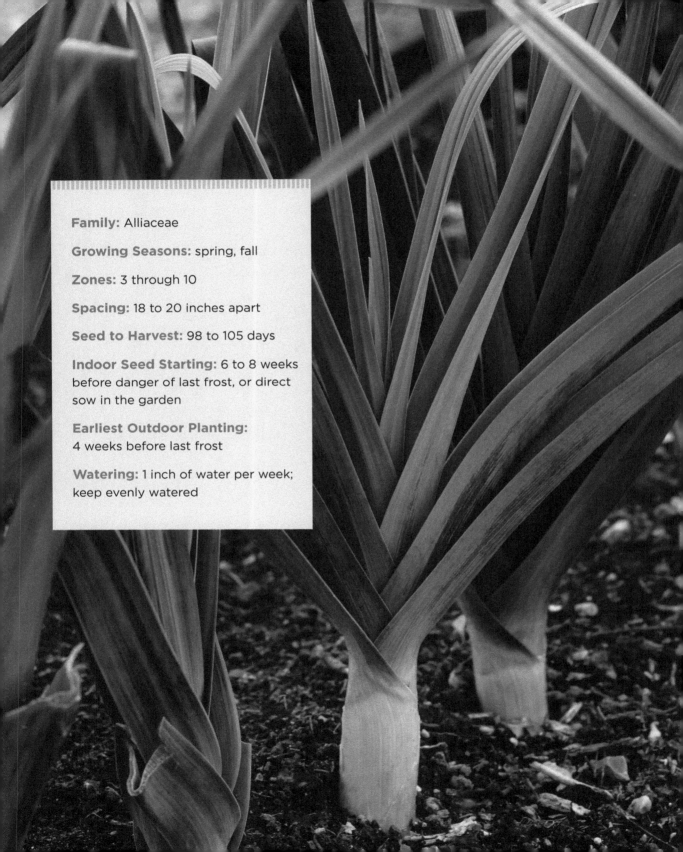

Family: Alliaceae

Growing Seasons: spring, fall

Zones: 3 through 10

Spacing: 18 to 20 inches apart

Seed to Harvest: 98 to 105 days

Indoor Seed Starting: 6 to 8 weeks before danger of last frost, or direct sow in the garden

Earliest Outdoor Planting: 4 weeks before last frost

Watering: 1 inch of water per week; keep evenly watered

LEEK

Allium porrum L.

Leeks grow through the winter in the Deep South. Some varieties are bred to overwinter in colder eastern climates.

Starting

Location: full sun, part shade

Growing

Leeks have a shallow root system and do best in a loose, well-drained soil. They should be kept well-watered and weeded. Mulching is a good way to hold the water and suppress the weeds. Avoid damaging when weeding or cultivating.

Harvesting

Leeks should be harvested when they are about 2 inches in diameter. Rock them back and forth to loosen them. Once harvested, the roots and all but 2 inches of the leaves should be cut off.

Problems

Damping off (pathogen-caused seedling collapse): Spray with a mixture of 1 tablespoon hydrogen peroxide per quart of water.

Downy mildew: Remove and discard affected parts of plants. Do not get water on leaves. Do increase airflow by thinning plants.

Family: Asteraceae

Growing Seasons: fall, summer, depending on zone; check your zone for specific times

Zones: 3 through 10

Spacing: 6 to 12 inches

Seed to Harvest: 45 to 75 days

Indoor Seed Starting: directly sow in the garden

Earliest Outdoor Planting: after danger of frost

Watering: water deeply at least once a week

LETTUCE

Lactuca sativa

Lettuce comes in leaf or head varieties, and each type offers diverse colors, shapes of leaves, and flavors to choose from.

Starting

Location: full sun in early spring; sow in shady areas in late summer in the South

Seeding: Do not start lettuce indoors. Plant it directly in your garden.

Planting: Cover seeds with ¼ inch of soil.

Growing

Weeding and watering are the only required maintenance. Keep lettuce well-watered during dry periods.

Harvesting

For leaf lettuce, harvest as desired. For head lettuce, harvest once heads are formed, cutting just below the crown.

Problems

Lettuce has shallow roots so be careful not to damage them when weeding, cultivating, or harvesting.

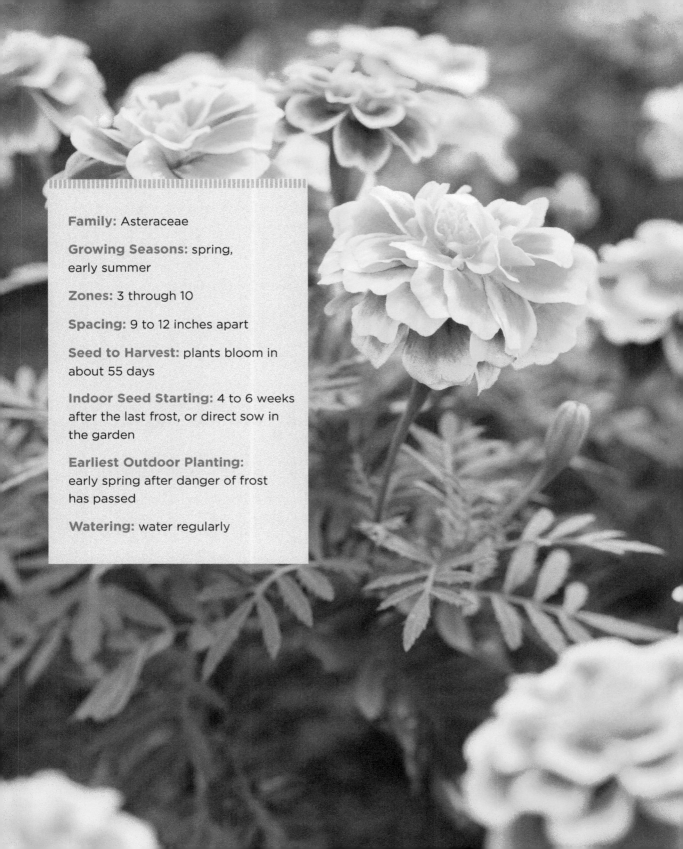

Family: Asteraceae

Growing Seasons: spring, early summer

Zones: 3 through 10

Spacing: 9 to 12 inches apart

Seed to Harvest: plants bloom in about 55 days

Indoor Seed Starting: 4 to 6 weeks after the last frost, or direct sow in the garden

Earliest Outdoor Planting: early spring after danger of frost has passed

Watering: water regularly

MARIGOLD

Tagetes

Marigolds are ornamental and not edible, but they are beautiful and help cut down on nematodes, beetles, and spider mites.

Starting

Location: full sun

Growing

Marigolds are quite easy to grow. They require only regular dead-heading—removal of dried and spent flowers. Reach beneath dead flowers and pinch them off the stem.

Harvesting

Marigolds are not harvested, because they are not an edible crop. You can cut marigolds and place them in a vase, but remove any leaves below the water.

Problems

Aphids: Use an insecticidal soap or a heavy spray of water to remove them.

Mites: Use an insecticidal soap or a heavy spray of water to remove them.

Fungal infections: These infections can occur if the soil is too wet. Apply a fungicide.

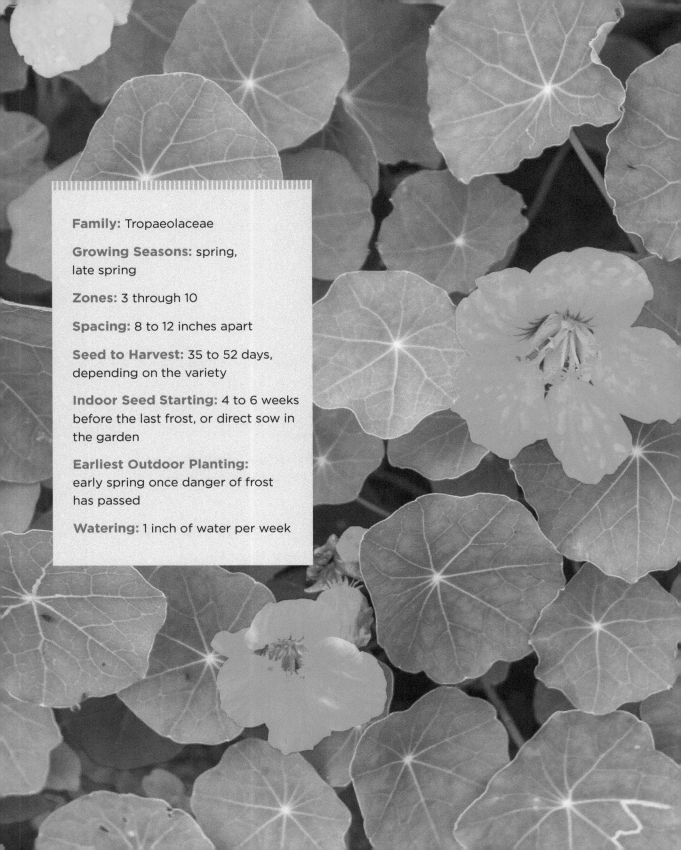

Family: Tropaeolaceae

Growing Seasons: spring, late spring

Zones: 3 through 10

Spacing: 8 to 12 inches apart

Seed to Harvest: 35 to 52 days, depending on the variety

Indoor Seed Starting: 4 to 6 weeks before the last frost, or direct sow in the garden

Earliest Outdoor Planting: early spring once danger of frost has passed

Watering: 1 inch of water per week

NASTURTIUM

Tropaeolum majus

Nasturtiums add color to your garden, and some are also edible. They are related to the watercress family.

Starting

Location: full sun

Planting: Plant seeds or seedlings after the danger of frost has passed.

Growing

Nasturtiums are available as a trailing grower, which can be trained up a trellis, or as a bush variety; read the description before ordering seeds. Soak seeds in water overnight before planting. Nasturtiums are notoriously low maintenance.

Harvesting

The flowers and leaves are edible. Use scissors to cut them off the plant. They have a strong peppery flavor, like watercress.

Problems

Aphids: Use an insecticidal soap or a heavy spray of water to remove them.

Cabbage butterflies: Remove them by hand.

Cucumber beetles: Remove them by hand.

Slugs: Remove them by hand.

White flies: Remove them by hand.

Family: Amaryllidaceae

Growing Seasons: spring, fall, depending on location; check your zone for specific times

Zones: 3 through 10

Spacing: 3 to 4 inches apart in rows 1 to 2 feet apart

Seed to Harvest: when planting seeds, 100 to 150 days; when planting seeds for green onions, 60 to 120 days; when planting onion sets (young plants), harvest at desired size as green onions or in 85 to 100 days as bulbs

Indoor Seed Starting: 6 to 10 weeks before the last spring frost

Earliest Outdoor Planting: after danger of heavy frost

Watering: keep the roots wet and tops dry; watering by ditch or drip irrigation is best

ONION

Allium cepa

Onions can be harvested as green onions or, if grown to full maturity, as bulbs.

Starting

Location: full sun

Planting: Plant onion sets by covering the bottom (white part). In the garden, cover the seeds with ¼ inch of soil. Short-day varieties are for the south and central United States; long-day varieties are for the north.

Transplant: Onions can be transplanted once the seedlings are about as thick as a pencil.

Growing

Because onions have shallow roots, give them adequate water at all times, by drip irrigation or a soaker hose. Do not get the tops wet.

Harvesting

Onion bulbs can be picked when their tops begin to turn yellow. Bend over the tops, wait several days, and then pull the bulbs. Dry onions in the garden for about 1 week or in a warm, dry location for 2 to 3 weeks.

Problems

Onions are usually pest-free. If you see yellow, drooping leaves before harvest, pull one and check for onion flies, which lay their eggs at the root. Use a floating row cover to protect seedlings.

Family: Apiaceae

Growing Seasons: spring or fall in frost-free zones

Zones: 3 through 10

Spacing: 12 inches apart

Seed to Harvest: 105 days

Indoor Seed Starting: not recommended

Earliest Outdoor Planting: early spring once your raised bed can be worked

Watering: 1 inch of water per week

PARSNIP

Pastinaca sativa

For the sweetest flavor, plant parsnips after a light frost.

Starting

Location: full sun, part shade

Growing

Mound soil around the shoulders of the plants to prevent the tops from turning green.

Harvesting

Get a good grip and pull.

Problems

Carrot weevil: Do not plant parsnips in the same location as carrots; practice crop rotation.

Leafhopper: Use a sticky trap.

Family: Fabaceae

Growing Seasons: in warmer climates, late winter; in cooler climates, early spring

Zones: 3 through 10

Spacing: 1 to 4 inches apart in rows 18 inches apart

Seed to Harvest: 68 to 75 days

Indoor Seed Starting: not recommended

Earliest Outdoor Planting: early spring once your raised bed can be worked

Watering: soil should be moist; heavy watering when the peas are flowering can decrease production

PEAS

Pisum sativum

Snow peas should be picked before the pod is full of enlarged peas. Shelling peas should be picked after the peas start to enlarge, but before they are ready to break open the pod.

Starting

Location: full sun, part shade (does best in full sun)

Planting: Plant peas 1 to 2 inches deep when the soil is cool and moist. If the soil is dry, plant them slightly deeper.

Growing

Peas should be grown on a trellis.

Harvesting

Peas are picked from the vine.

Problems

Aphids: Use an insecticidal soap or a heavy spray of water to remove them.

Powdery mildew: Spray the affected areas with a solution of 2 to 3 tablespoons of white vinegar per gallon of water.

True wilt (Fusarium) and near wilt: Use fungicide.

Family: Solanaceae

Growing Seasons: spring, fall

Zones: 3 through 10; plant early potatoes (these mature in fewer than 90 days) in zones 9 and 10

Spacing: plant in a trench 6 to 8 inches deep; place seed potatoes at 12 to 18 inches; allow 2 to 3 feet between rows

Seed to Harvest: 70 to 120 days, depending on the variety

Indoor Seed Starting: you can grow potatoes indoors, from seed to maturity, but don't plant seeds indoors and then transplant them outdoors; seeds should be planted directly in the ground

Earliest Outdoor Planting: 1 to 2 weeks before the last frost; you can plant some varieties in zone 9 and up in the fall

Watering: water regularly without saturating the soil

POTATO

Solanum tuberosum

Purchase seed potatoes from a nursery. Do not use potatoes from the grocery; they have been treated to prevent sprouting.

Starting

Location: full sun; requires at least 6 hours of sunlight per day

Planting: Cut the seed potatoes into pieces; each must have an "eye" (root). Plant the pieces with the eye up.

Growing

Potatoes like a pH of 5 to 5.5. You can plant potatoes in the ground or in specialized containers.

Harvesting

Harvest new potatoes (those that will be used immediately) when the plants begin to flower. Harvest potatoes for storing when the plant leaves have turned yellow and are starting to dry out. You can harvest potatoes with a shovel, but a garden fork works best.

Problems

Potatoes may be affected by beetles or aphids. Use a row cover if you see flea beetles. You may need to use BT (*Bacillus thuringiensis*) for Colorado potato beetles. Read the instructions on the BT label and apply the BT accordingly.

Family: Brassicaceae

Growing Seasons: spring, fall

Zones: 3 through 10

Spacing: 3 to 4 inches apart

Seed to Harvest: 30 to 60 days

Indoor Seed Starting: not recommended

Earliest Outdoor Planting: early spring once your raised bed can be worked

Watering: 1 inch of water per week

RADISH

Raphanus sativus

Radishes taste better when they are grown in cool weather. Once the temperature goes above 65 degrees Fahrenheit, they develop a spicier taste.

Starting

Location: full sun

Planting: In most areas, radishes can be grown in early spring and again in late fall.

Growing

Do not overfertilize.

Harvesting

Pull radishes once their bulbs have reached the desired size; if grown too long, they become pithy.

Problems

Cabbage root maggots: Do not plant radishes in the same location again; practice crop rotation.

Clubroot: Remove affected plants.

Family: Polygonaceae

Growing Seasons: spring, late fall in warmer climates

Zones: 3 through 8

Spacing: 3 to 4 feet apart

Seed to Harvest: 365 days to maturity

Indoor Seed Starting: not recommended

Earliest Outdoor Planting: early spring

Watering: 1 inch of water per week

RHUBARB

Rheum rhabarbarum

Rhubarb needs extended temperatures below 40 degrees Fahrenheit. The plants thrive in colder climates and can live up to 15 years. In beds, rhubarb plants should be divided sometime between years 5 and 15, basically when they need to be thinned. Do not eat the leaves—they are toxic. Only eat the stalks.

Starting

Location: full sun, part shade

Planting: Plant bare-root plants. Plants require little to no fertilizer.

Growing

Remove flower stalks in the first year.

Harvesting

Leave at least one-third of the plant when harvesting; doing so will strengthen the plant.

Problems

Rhubarb is relatively pest- and disease-free.

Family: Amaranthaceae

Growing Seasons: fall, spring

Zones: 3 through 10

Spacing: 4 inches

Seed to Harvest: 30 to 44 days

Indoor Seed Starting: directly sow in the garden

Earliest Outdoor Planting: early in spring; no need to wait for last frost

Watering: needs 1 to 1½ inches of water per week during the growth cycle

SPINACH

Spinacia oleracea

Harvest young leaves as desired. Once the weather starts to warm, harvest the entire plant.

Use bolt-resistant varieties in warmer climates.

Starting

Location: full sun, part sun

Planting: Cover the seeds with ½ inch of soil.

Growing

Weeding and watering are the only needed maintenance.

Harvesting

Cut spinach as desired.

Problems

Spinach has few problems when grown properly in cool weather.

Family: Cucurbitaceae

Growing Seasons: early spring to early summer

Zones: 3 through 10

Spacing: 3 to 4 feet apart

Seed to Harvest: 40 to 55 days

Indoor Seed Starting: 3 to 4 weeks before transplanting, or directly sow in the garden

Earliest Outdoor Planting: do not plant until the soil reaches 65 degrees Fahrenheit

Watering: 1 to 2 inches of water per week

SQUASH

Cucurbita pepo

Squash have both male and female flowers on the same plant, so they self-pollinate.

Starting

Location: full sun

Planting: Squash prefer a soil temperature higher than 65 degrees Fahrenheit.

Growing

Weeding and watering are the only needed maintenance.

Harvesting

Twist the squash off the vine when they reach the desired size.

Problems

Squash bug: Remove manually.

Squash vine borer: Use neem oil.

Striped cucumber beetles: Use neem oil.

Powdery mildew: Spray affected areas with a solution of 2 to 3 tablespoons of white vinegar per gallon of water.

Family: Asteraceae

Growing Seasons: spring,
late spring

Zones: 3 through 10

Spacing: 18 to 24 inches

Seed to Harvest: 70 to 90 days

Indoor Seed Starting: directly sow
in the garden

Earliest Outdoor Planting: after
danger of frost

Watering: soil should be moist,
but not wet

SUNFLOWER

Helianthus

Harvest sunflower seeds for your own enjoyment, or leave them for your backyard birds and squirrels.

Starting

Location: full sun

Seeding: Do not start sunflowers indoors. Plant them directly in the garden.

Planting: Cover seeds with ½ inch of soil. Plant taller varieties north of shorter plants so they don't shade the shorter plants.

Growing

Weeding and watering are the only needed maintenance. Sunflowers do not require fertilizer if grown in good garden soil. Once the flower is growing, it can handle drought-type conditions.

Harvesting

Sunflowers are ready for harvest once their heads start to droop and their stalks are dry. Cut the heads with 1 foot of stem attached. Hang them in an area with good air circulation until the seeds are dry and ready to eat.

Problems

Some bugs, including beetles, cutworms, and moths, may affect your sunflowers if their growing area is not kept clean and weed-free. If you end up with a problem, apply the human- and pet-safe BT (*Bacillus thuringiensis*) bacterium as directed on the BT label.

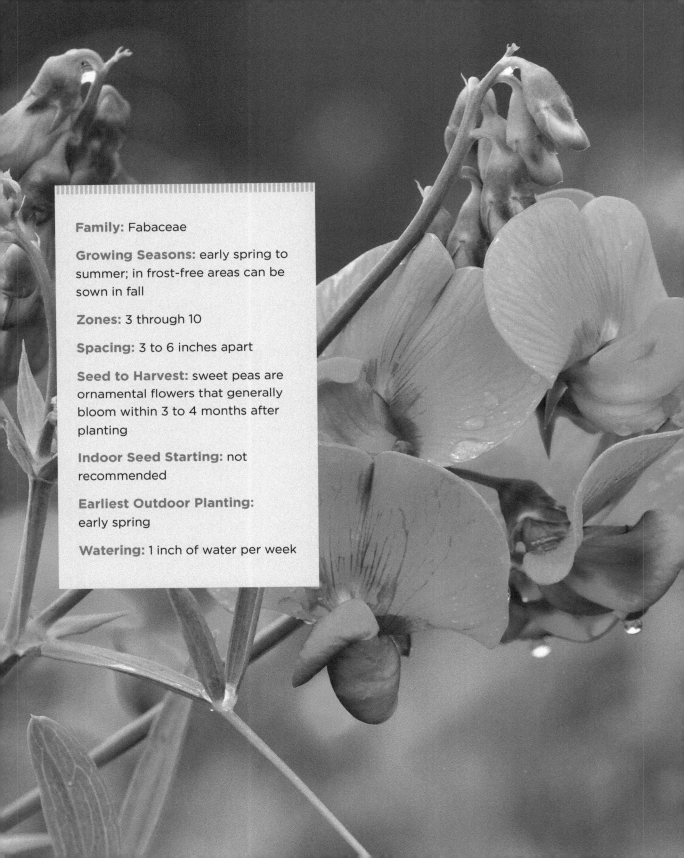

Family: Fabaceae

Growing Seasons: early spring to summer; in frost-free areas can be sown in fall

Zones: 3 through 10

Spacing: 3 to 6 inches apart

Seed to Harvest: sweet peas are ornamental flowers that generally bloom within 3 to 4 months after planting

Indoor Seed Starting: not recommended

Earliest Outdoor Planting: early spring

Watering: 1 inch of water per week

SWEET PEA

L. odoratus

Sweet peas are great for borders and lovely as cut flowers. They are not edible.

Starting

Location: full sun

Planting: Soak seeds in water overnight before sowing. Sweet peas can tolerate a light frost.

Growing

Sweet peas are climbing plants and will need a trellis or some other support. Some dwarf sweet peas do not need the support.

Harvesting

Once the lowest blossom barely opens, cut the stems any time you like. Frequent picking means the plants put their energy into growing more fragrant, beautiful blooms. Regularly deadhead sweet peas to keep them in production.

Problems

Slugs: Remove them by hand.

Powdery mildew: Spray affected areas with a solution of 2 to 3 table-spoons of white vinegar per gallon of water.

Family: Solanaceae

Growing Seasons: April through October, depending on location

Zones: 3 through 10

Spacing: plant tomato plants 3 feet apart in rows 3 feet apart; in a 4-by-4-foot bed, you can plant a maximum of 4 plants, one in each corner; keep them far enough away from the corner so you can trellis them or use a tomato cage

Seed to Harvest: 65 to 85 days

Indoor Seed Starting: 6 to 8 weeks before the last frost

Earliest Outdoor Planting: after the last frost

Watering: water regularly; irregular watering may cause problems such as blossom end rot; tomatoes need at least 1 inch of water per week

TOMATO

Solanum lycopersicum

Do not try to plant tomato seeds outdoors. Most areas do not have long enough growing seasons to harvest tomatoes grown in this manner. Either start your own seedlings or purchase seedlings from a local nursery.

Tomato plants are either determinate or indeterminate. Most of us grow indeterminate tomato plants, which have blossoms, immature fruit, and mature fruit on the plant all at the same time. They average 6 feet in height but can grow to 12 feet. Determinate plants are bush-type plants that are 3 to 4 feet high, and all their fruit ripens at the same time. They require limited staking and are great for container and raised-bed gardening.

Most tomatoes will not set (make fruit) when it is below 55 degrees Fahrenheit at night. They prefer 60- to 90-degree temperatures during the day, but temperatures higher than 90 degrees during the day will decrease (or halt) production. Some varieties, such as Celebrity, Oregon Spring, and Bush Beefsteak Tomato, will set at cooler temperatures.

Starting

Location: full sun; requires at least 8 hours of sunlight per day

Planting: Plant tomato seedlings with the stem laying sideways. Roots will form along the stem. Plant them deep, leaving about the top third of the seedling exposed. They will grow "up" toward the sun and become upright. Be careful not to damage the stem when placing your cages or stakes around them.

(Continued)

TOMATO *(Continued)*

Growing

Remove suckers, which form in the area between two branches. They will not produce tomatoes.

Prune tomatoes lightly to remove some leaves, thereby increasing the plants' sun exposure.

Harvesting

Pick green or slightly pink tomatoes for dishes such as fried green tomatoes. Do not refrigerate tomatoes. Store them on the counter until you are ready to eat or process them.

Problems

Hornworms: Remove them manually. These pests can be hard to spot, because they are the same color as tomato leaves. You will know they are an issue when you see holes in your leaves and insect droppings.

Blossom end rot: This brown spot on the bottom of the tomato can be avoided with regular plant watering. The rot may disappear as the season continues. Cut around the spot and eat the rest of the tomato.

Family: Cucurbitaceae, also called curbits

Growing Seasons: spring, late spring

Zones: 3 through 10

Spacing: 36 inches

Seed to Harvest: 40 to 50 days

Indoor Seed Starting: directly sow in the garden

Earliest Outdoor Planting: after danger of frost

Watering: needs 1 to 2 inches of water per week during the growth cycle

ZUCCHINI

Cucurbita pepo

Squash plants have both male and female flowers, so they self-pollinate.

Starting

Location: full sun

Planting: Cover seeds with 1 inch of soil when planting them directly in the garden.

Growing

Weeding and watering are the only needed maintenance.

Harvesting

Cut the mature, hard vegetable off the vine.

Problems

Lack of bees or pollinators can lead to lack of zucchini. You may need to hand-pollinate if you are not getting fruit. You must wait until male and female flowers are present to hand-pollinate. The male flowers, which will be the first to appear on your plants, have a stem that looks the same from the vine to the blossom. The female flowers have a small zucchini at their base below the flower. Cut a male flower at the stem and transfer the pollen from its interior to the interior of the female flowers, covering the female flowers' centers in pollen. You can use one male plant to pollinate up to three female flowers.

RESOURCES

Burpee.com

Burpee is an excellent seed company with a large selection of vegetables, flowers, herbs, heirlooms, and fruit. I have been purchasing seeds from them for years. Request a free catalog and shop online, or call 1-800-888-1447.

Directory for County Extension Offices

Your local extension agent can offer valuable, often free, help. He or she can help you identify pests and diseases, provide soil testing (for a nominal charge), and share vegetable planting guidelines for your area. See https://nifa.usda.gov/land-grant-colleges-and-universities-partner-website-directory.

Frameitall.com

Frame It All sells materials for simple modular gardens, including corner joints, composite boards, and stacking corners. Its kits and accessories also can be found at Lowe's and Home Depot.

Lehmans.com

This family-owned business in an Amish community in Ohio offers a large selection of seeds and gardening items. It also sells canning and preserving tools and low-tech items that work just as well today as they did when my grandmother was using them. Request a free catalog and shop online, or call 1-800-438-5346.

Parkseed.com

Park's sells a large selection of vegetables, flowers, herbs, heirlooms, and fruit, and I have been purchasing seeds from this company for a long time. Request a free catalog and shop online, or call 1-800-845-3369.

YellaWood.com

YellaWood's pressure-treated boards are safe for raised-bed garden projects. The boards are available at hardware stores and lumberyards; use the directory on the YellaWood site to find a dealer. Get a free plan for a raised bed on the site at https://bit.ly/2TE9rWG.

PLANT HARDINESS ZONES

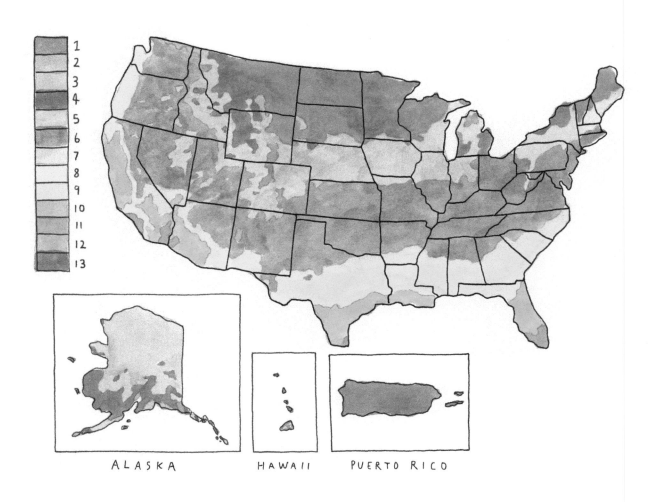

1
2
3
4
5
6
7
8
9
10
11
12
13

ALASKA

HAWAII

PUERTO RICO

INDEX

ABOUT THE AUTHOR

TAMMY WYLIE is a lifelong gardener who has been involved in selling, designing, and installing greenhouses since 1993. She opened the online retailer Advance Greenhouses (advancegreenhouses.com) in 2002. The company sells greenhouse kits, greenhouse accessories, and gardening items. Tammy answers the phone most days and has had many interesting conversations with fellow gardeners. In 2018, Tammy started blogging at growyourownfoodanywhere. com. The name perfectly describes the blog's mission: growing food in an apartment, in a small rental house, on a balcony, in raised-bed gardens on acreage, in a greenhouse—anywhere. A regular contributor to *Garden & Greenhouse* magazine, Tammy was recognized as a Top Writer 2018 in the gardening niche on Quora.com.

Printed in the USA
CPSIA information can be obtained
at www.ICGtesting.com
CBHW040524020624
9266CB00002BA/4